2i3D

Wasatch 3D Atlas

First Edition

Printed in the United States of America

ISBN: 978-0-9825020-3-7

This book is distributed by
Brigham Distributing
110 South 800 West
Brigham City, Utah 84302
Website *brighamdistributing.com*
Email *brigdist@sisna.com*
Telephone 435-723-6611
Fax 435-723-6644

Also available from 2i3D, *3D Atlas of Zion National Park*.
Go to www.2i3d.com for more products.

Lake Blanche in Big Cottonwood Canyon

When Mormon pioneers entered the Salt Lake Valley in 1847, it was mostly uninhabited. The area was a disputed boundary that separated three groups of Indians. The Shoshone and Bannock Indians lived to the north, the Goshutes to the west, and the Utes lived near Utah Lake to the south. When the area was surveyed under the leadership of US Army explorer Howard Stansbury in 1849-50, his map included the original Ute Indian names of these places. City Creek was known as Nah-po-pah, Parleys Creek was Obit-ke-ke-che, Mill Creek was Ombit-o-pah, Big Cottonwood Creek was We-en-de-quint, and Little Cottonwood Creek was Wa-ko-ne-kin.* The proximity of these creeks to the Salt Lake Valley made them known and appreciated by Native Americans for hundreds of years prior to pioneer times. The canyons were an early source of water, timber, and building stone, as well as fish and game. The pioneers who settled this area took advantage of those resources on a much larger scale, and later developments include mining, camping, rock climbing, biking, skiing, and snowboarding.

The maps in this book are presented as anaglyphs, which are currently the best way to easily present large 3D maps in print. The index map on pages 6 and 7 gives an idea of what area each of the maps covers. For the rest of the book, a small index diagram is included to help you find adjacent maps by page number. Except for maps on facing pages, each sheet overlaps its neighbors by ¼ mile (402 meters).

Inside the cover of this book is a pocket containing two pairs of 3D anaglyphic glasses. It is recommended that you avoid touching the lenses of these glasses and attempt to keep them clean. The maps should be viewed while wearing the glasses with the red lens over your left eye. We suggest that the anaglyph glasses only be worn when you are looking at the maps. If the glasses are worn for extended periods of time, some people may experience a temporary difficulty adapting to natural colors upon removing them. Those who wear prescription glasses may be able to wear the anaglyph glasses over or under them. It has been determined that about 1 in 10 people are unable to see 3D. Unfortunately, this book will be of little benefit to them.

The map on each page is actually two maps that are printed on top of each other in contrasting colors. Though they cover the exact same area, the maps are not identical. If you look at the page through the red lens, you will see one of these maps. The opposite of red is cyan, and through that lens you will see the other map. If you look at the left and right borders of the map you can see that both images have been distorted to the right or left to resemble perspective views. The cyan image is only visible through the red filter, and the red image is only visible through the cyan filter. That's the ideal case; the filters and inks used in printing the anaglyphs don't work together perfectly, so it should be normal to see a faint ghost image, especially in areas of high contrast. The colored plastic filters reduce the amount of light that reaches your eyes, so the 3D effect will be easiest to see if you view the maps in a well-lit area.

The vertical scale is an approximation, based on a page that is viewed from 10 inches away, by eyes that are 2.5 inches apart. Since the maps are at a scale of 1 inch to ½ mile, or 2640 feet, this is similar to what you would see if you were a towering giant with eyes that are 6600 feet apart, looking vertically down on the area from a distance of 26,400 feet above the highest point. As you view the page from farther away you will notice that the relief becomes more pronounced, and you should be able to settle on a preferred distance from which to view the page.

The Wasatch Mountains are among the most beautiful places in Utah. This book gives a good idea, at a glance, of the rugged topography that can be found in these canyons and the mountains that separate them. You should always keep in mind that there are many hazards that the map is unable to depict, and the ultimate responsibility for any decision you make or route you take is yours. The maps in this book may provide you with useful information, but we are unable to assume responsibility for decisions you might make while consulting these maps, so please be careful up there.

How This Book Was Made

Since its inception in 1879, the United States Geological Survey (USGS) has had a goal of mapping the entire country at scales that would make the maps useful to geologists, engineers, and the general public. Beginning in the early 1940s and continuing through the remainder of the 20th Century, the Geological Survey took on the ambitious project of mapping the entire country in a series of maps called quadrangles. Each quadrangle covers a shape of 7½ minutes square, totaling nearly 57,000 map sheets , at a scale of 1:24,000. This means that 1 inch on the map equals 24,000 inches on the ground, or 2,000 feet. There are 64 quadrangles in one square geographic degree. They are called quadrangles because they replaced an earlier map format, with four quadrangles covering the same area as one 15-minute sheet, usually scaled at 1:62,500. Each of the maps in most cases is named after a prominent feature within its borders. For this book we selected a scale of 1:31,680 and used all or part of 23 7½ minute quadrangles (see the map on page 48).

The quadrangles used in this book were originally created by the Geological Survey in 1950 from aerial photographs using a method called photogrammetry, combined with extensive ground surveys and field checking. Because of the area's proximity to Salt Lake City, enough changes had occurred in the canyons to require some revisions to the maps, which took place in 1977. Then, in 1995, Salt Lake City was selected as the site for the 2002 Winter Olympics, and in 1998 the maps were updated by the US Forest Service to serve the planning needs for that event. The Forest Service added additional features to support its purposes, such as outlining properties within the National Forest that are privately owned, marking picnic areas and campgrounds with special symbols, and numbering trails. Digital versions of the maps, in GeoTIFF format, were obtained from the US Forest Service's Geometronics Service Center. These maps only exist for areas that contain Forest Service properties, so three of the maps we used were obtained from the US Geological Survey (Wanship, Park City East, and Heber City).

The Geological Survey also used scanned maps to create Digital Elevation Models, or DEMs. These are simply an array of elevations, evenly spaced and formatted so that the computer can quickly read them. Areas to the east of the yellow line on page 48 were made from 10 meter USGS DEMs, while areas to the west used 6 meter 2006 LiDAR data from the Utah Automated Geographic Reference Center (AGRC). Each map in this atlas was created from about 1.6 million elevation points. For comparison, each map image covering the same area consists of about 8 million pixels.

A Digital Elevation Model has many uses, and can be displayed in a variety of ways. It can be combined with the topographic map to add relief shading (Fig. 1), but it can do other things as well. Figure 2 shows a DEM using levels of brightness and darkness to illustrate that the computer recognizes which points on the model are higher than the others. Utilizing this information, the computer creates a second image in which each pixel of the original map has been shifted to a new location based on its elevation. The resulting image has been transformed by this process to resemble a perspective view.

Fig. 1

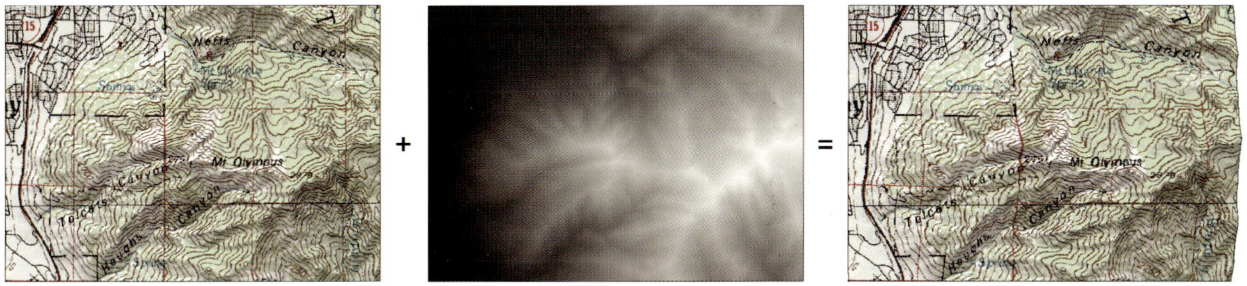

Fig. 2

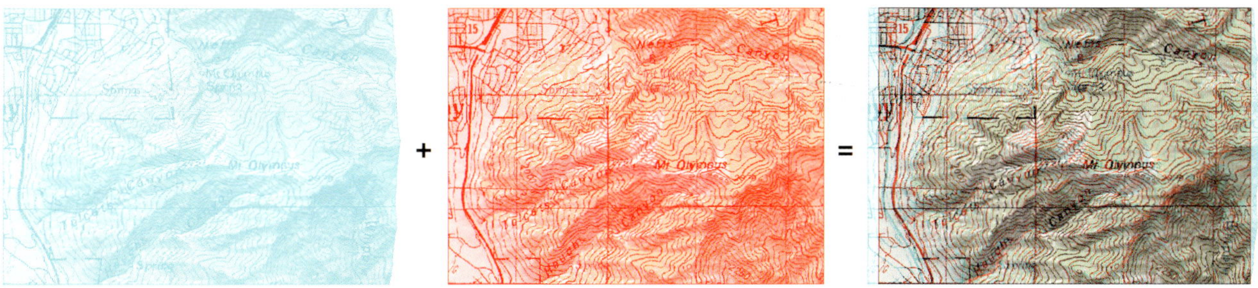

Fig. 3

By use of computer software, it is possible to take the color perspective images apart to create three images, each composed of only the colors red, green, or blue. A composite image can then be created that combines the red image from one perspective view with the green and blue images from the other view. When the image is viewed through the glasses, each eye sees only one of the two perspective images (Fig. 3). These nine images provide a simplified visual explanation of how a map is transformed into anaglyphic 3D.

A topographic map only shows features that existed at the time it was made. It includes such things as roads and trails, boundaries, names of canyons and lakes, and a series of imaginary lines called contours, which connect points on the ground that have the same elevation. These are features that the mapmakers added to make the map useful to you. Both images have been distorted to create the 3D effect. When you wear the glasses, some of the peaks will appear to be an inch or more above the surface of the page; other features will seem to be below the surface. The amount of offset applied depends on the vertical distance above or below the model's average elevation.

This book could not have been made without the anaglyphic capabilities of a Geographic Information System (GIS) called Microdem, written by Professor Peter Guth of the US Naval Academy. Terrain texture was added using a process developed by Leland Brown. The images were further groomed using various kinds of image editing software, especially Adobe Photoshop, Adobe Illustrator, and Corel Paint Shop Pro. We also used a program known as Stereo Photo Maker, written by Masuji Suto of Ryugasaki, Ibaraki, Japan. A part of Mr. Suto's program uses an algorithm by Professor Eric Dubois of the University of Ottawa in Canada that was useful in adjusting the colors to make them suitable as anaglyphs. We are also grateful to Mr. David Romeuf of Clermont-Ferrand, France for sharing the results of his extensive research into improving the methods for printing anaglyphs using a subtractive process. The illustrations on the cover and the first page were created using Natural Scene Designer Pro 7.0 software from Natural Graphics.

We hope that making these maps available in realistic color 3D will provide you with a new method for understanding, appreciating, and enjoying the mountain landscapes that are just minutes away from the populated areas in the valley of the Great Salt Lake.

*Myron Accuttoroop of the Ute Tribe believes Ombit-o-pah means "Big Water." We-en-de-quint means "Little Water Running." He was unable to determine the meaning of Wa-ko-ne-kin, and suspects it might not be a Ute word, as there were also Shoshone and Bannock Indians in the area when the Mormons arrived in 1847. The Goshute or Gosiute Indians of western Utah also had names for the creeks: Mill Creek was known as Tin'go-u-pi, meaning "Rock Trap," because it contains a cliff over which game animals could be driven to their deaths, Big Cottonwood Creek was Pi'a-bai-gwi-ci, or "Big Torrent," while Little Cottonwood Creek was Si'a-dai-di-ma, the meaning of which was not given. See Ralph V. Chamberlin, Place and personal names of the Gosiute Indians of Utah, *Proceedings of the American Philosophical Society*, Vol. 52, No. 208, 1913, pp. 1-20.

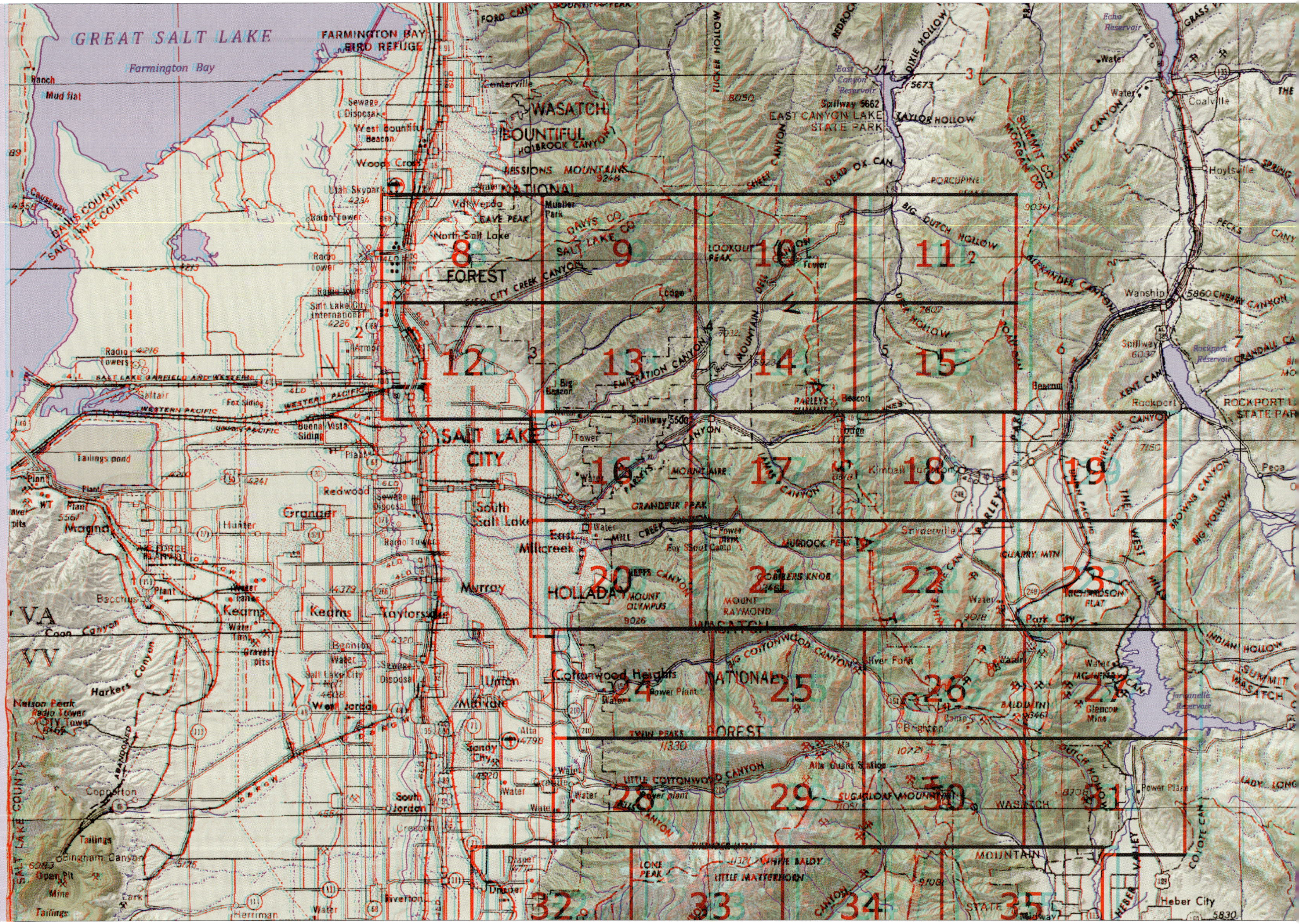

The anaglyph X displacement is 751 feet (229 meters), centered at 6421 feet (1957 meters) between the low elevation of 4210 feet and the high elevation of 7209 feet (1283 to 2197 meters).

N

SCALE 1 : 250 000

0 5 10 MILES

0 5 10 15 KILOMETERS

UTAH

Index North

L R

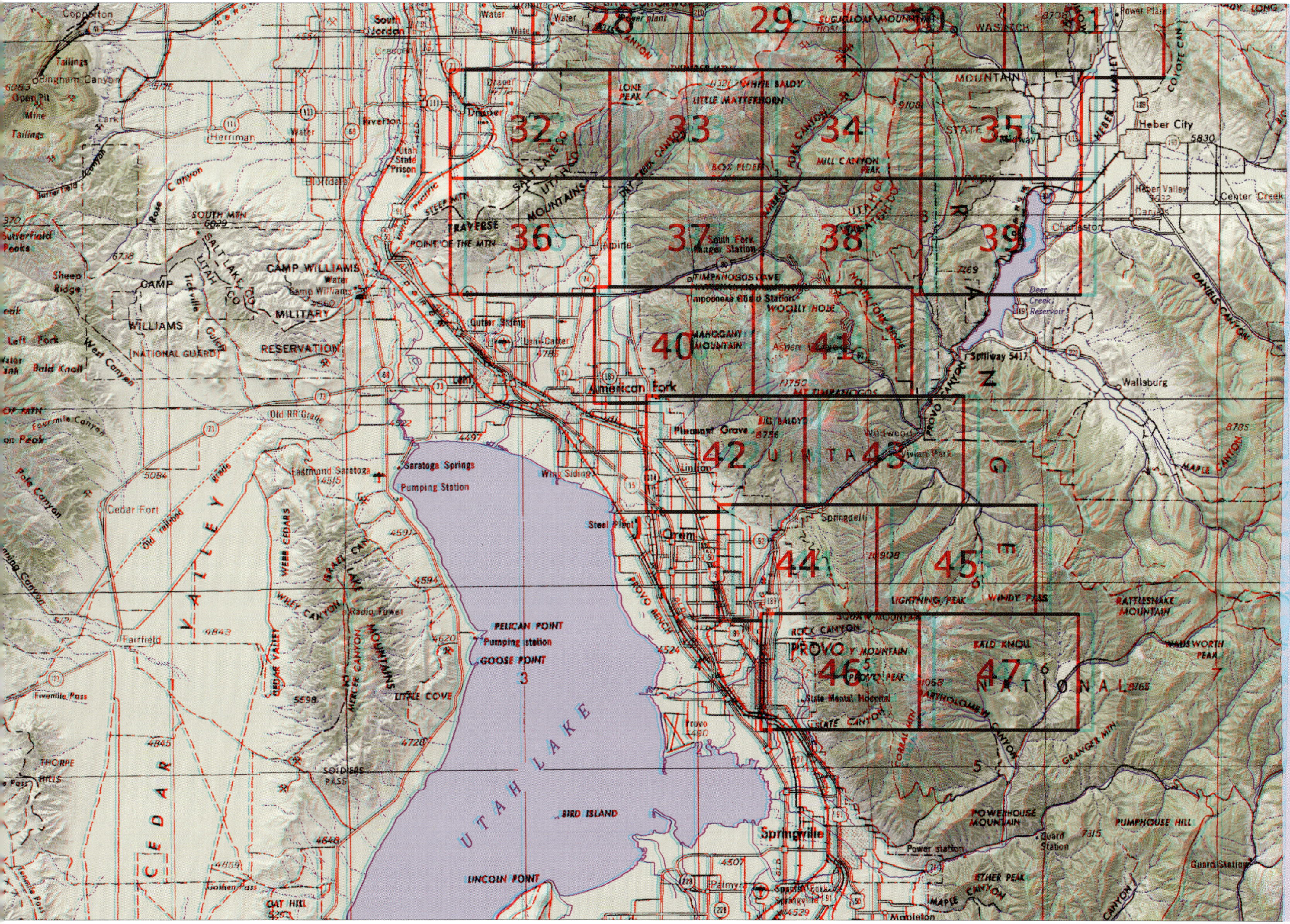

The anaglyph X displacement is 994 feet (303 meters), centered at 6421 feet (1957 meters) between the low elevation of 5443 feet and the high elevation of 9419 feet (1659 to 2871 meters).

N

SCALE 1 : 250 000

0 5 10 MILES

0 5 10 15 KILOMETERS

UTAH

Index South

L R

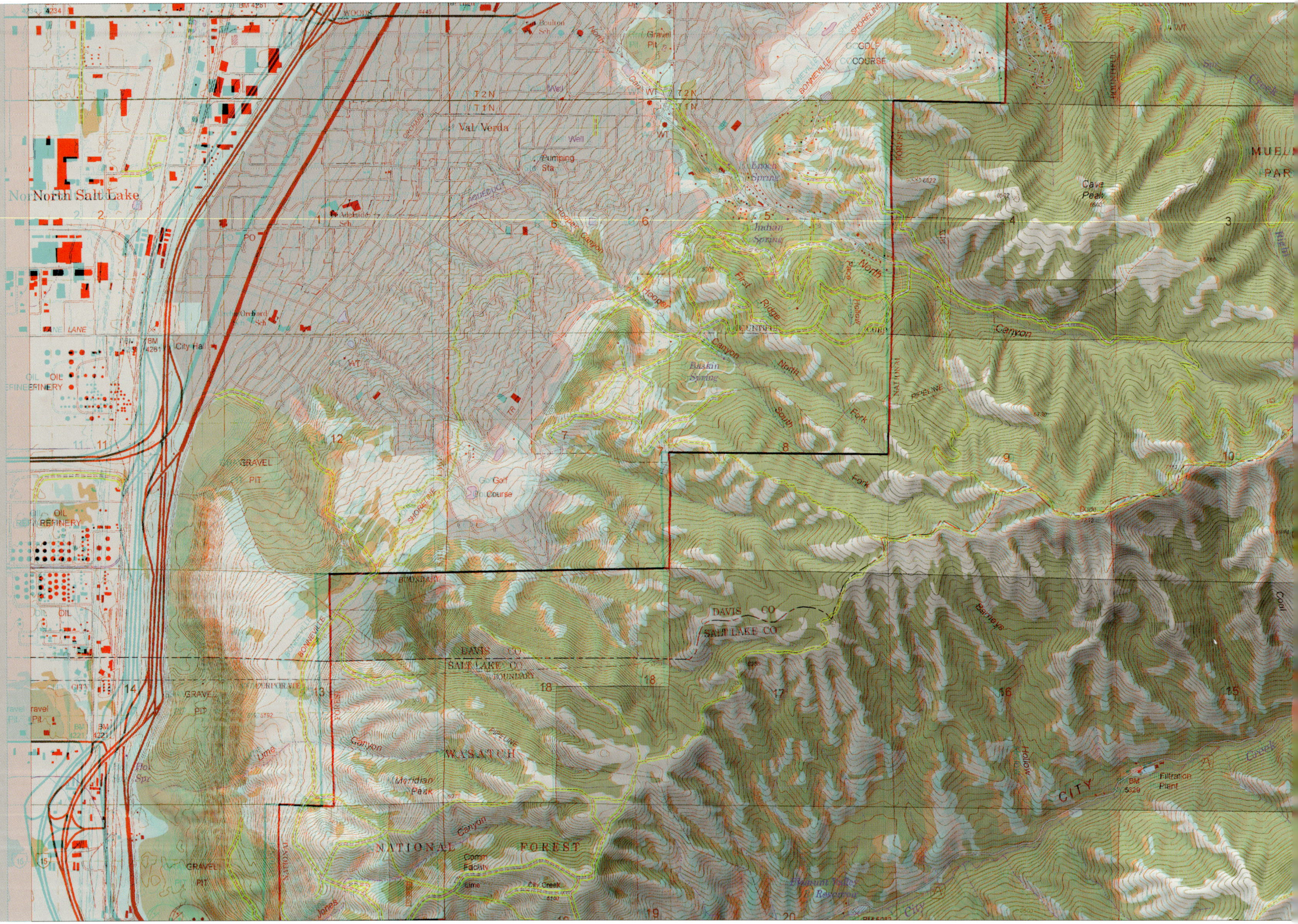

The anaglyph X displacement is 751 feet (229 meters), centered at 6421 feet (1957 meters) between the low elevation of 4210 feet and the high elevation of 7209 feet (1283 to 2197 meters).

8	9
12	13

ADJACENT PAGES

N

SCALE 1 INCH = ½ MILE

0 ½ 1 MILE

0 1000 2000 3000 4000 FEET

0 0.5 1 KILOMETER

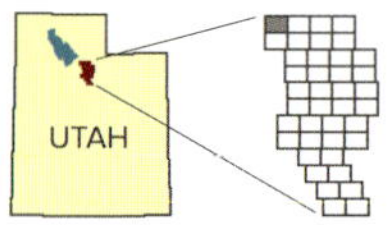

Meridian Peak

L R

The anaglyph X displacement is 994 feet (303 meters), centered at 6421 feet (1957 meters) between the low elevation of 5443 feet and the high elevation of 9419 feet (1659 to 2871 meters).

8	9	10
12	13	14

ADJACENT PAGES

N

SCALE 1 INCH = ½ MILE

0 ½ 1 MILE

0 1000 2000 3000 4000 FEET

0 0.5 1 KILOMETER

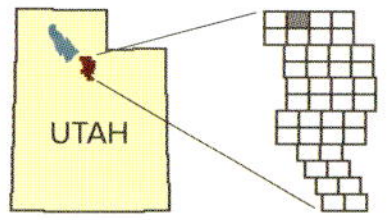

Rotary Park

L R

The anaglyph X displacement is 709 feet (216 meters), centered at 7116 feet (2169 meters) between the low elevation of 6123 feet and the high elevation of 8961 feet (1866 to 2731 meters).

9	10	11
13	14	15

ADJACENT PAGES

SCALE 1 INCH = ½ MILE

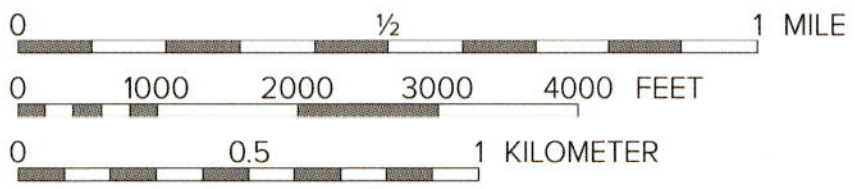

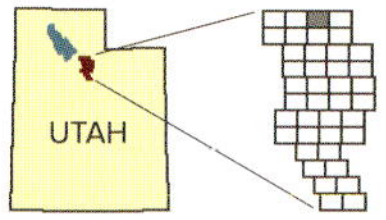

Big Mountain Pass

L R

The anaglyph X displacement is 659 feet (201 meters), centered at 7116 feet (2169 meters) between the low elevation of 5767 feet and the high elevation of 8407 feet (1758 to 2563 meters).

10	11
14	15

ADJACENT PAGES

N

SCALE 1 INCH = ½ MILE

0 ½ 1 MILE

0 1000 2000 3000 4000 FEET

0 0.5 1 KILOMETER

UTAH

Mormon Flat

L R

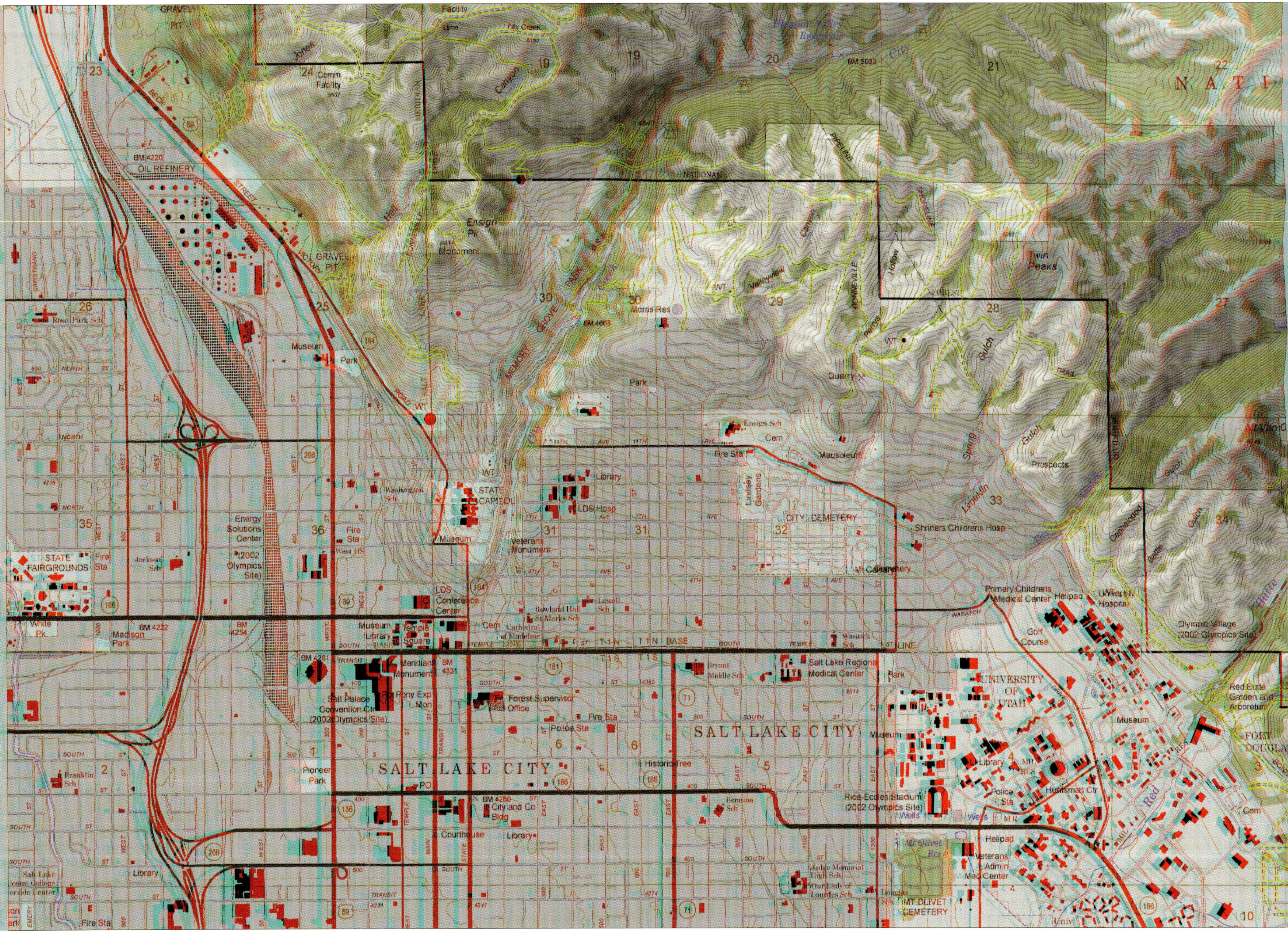

The anaglyph X displacement is 607 feet (185 meters), centered at 5525 feet (1684 meters) between the low elevation of 4209 feet and the high elevation of 6642 feet (1283 to 2025 meters).

8	9
12	13
	16

ADJACENT PAGES

N

SCALE 1 INCH = ½ MILE

0 ½ 1 MILE

0 1000 2000 3000 4000 FEET

0 0.5 1 KILOMETER

UTAH

Memory Grove

L R

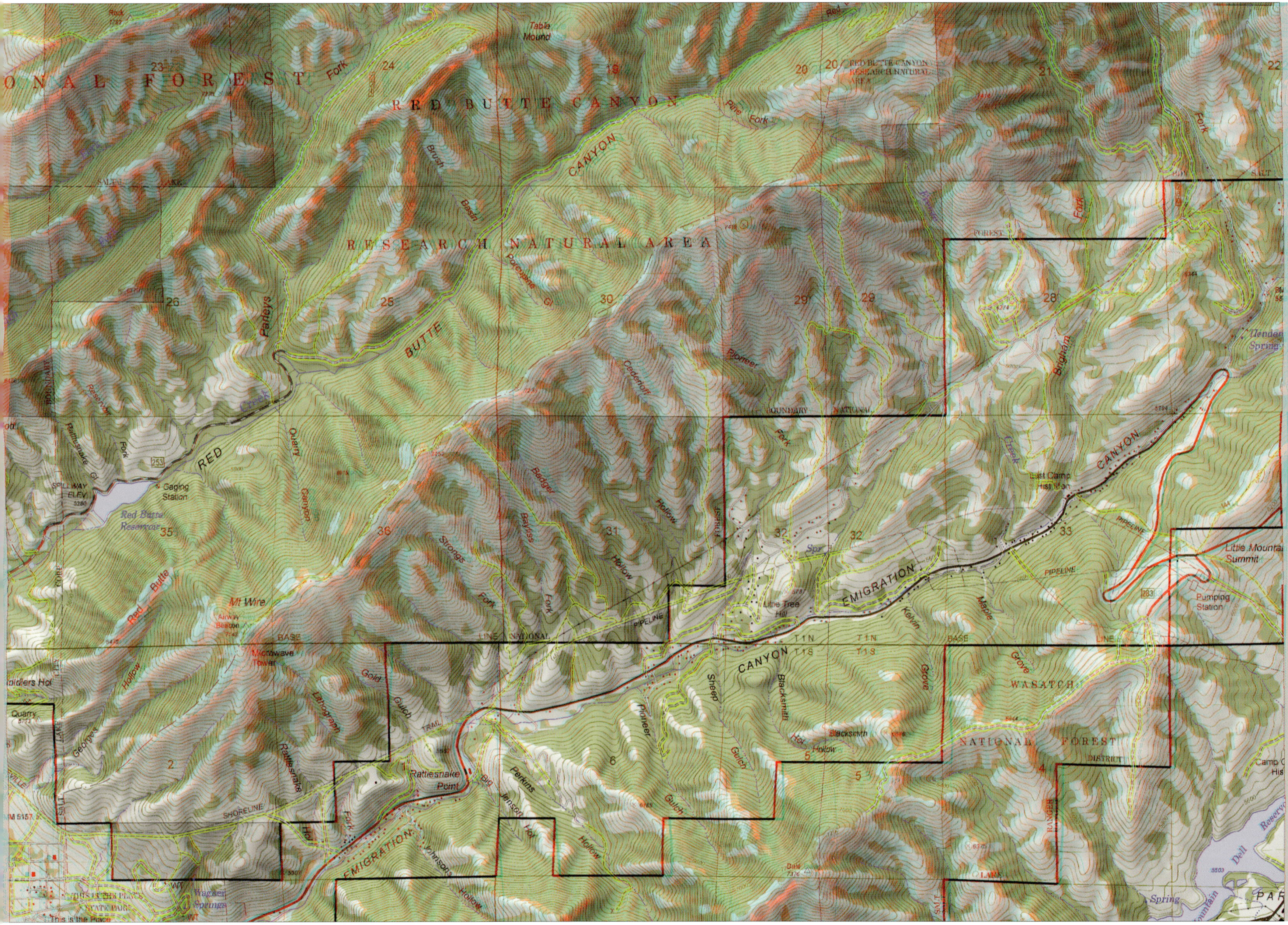

The anaglyph X displacement is 741 feet (226 meters), centered at 5525 feet (1684 meters) between the low elevation of 4852 feet and the high elevation of 7812 feet (1479 to 2381 meters).

8	9	10
12	13	14
	16	17

ADJACENT PAGES

N

SCALE 1 INCH = ½ MILE

0 ½ 1 MILE

0 1000 2000 3000 4000 FEET

0 0.5 1 KILOMETER

UTAH

Red Butte Canyon

L R

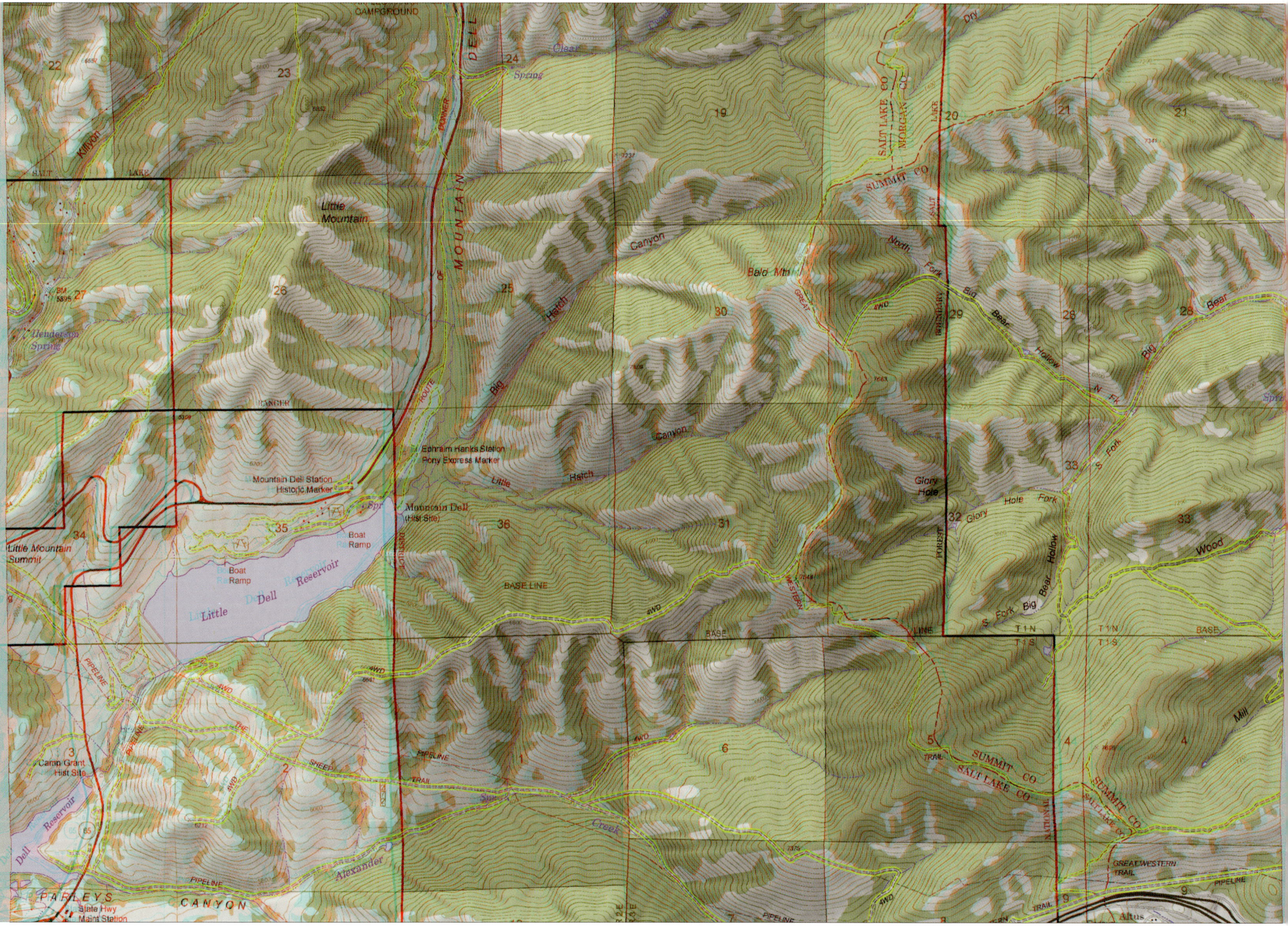

The anaglyph X displacement is 587 feet (179 meters), centered at 6788 feet (2069 meters) between the low elevation of 5504 feet and the high elevation of 7858 feet (1678 to 2395 meters).

9	10	11
13	14	15
16	17	18

ADJACENT PAGES

N

SCALE 1 INCH = ½ MILE

0 ½ 1 MILE

0 1000 2000 3000 4000 FEET

0 0.5 1 KILOMETER

UTAH

Little Mountain

L R

The anaglyph X displacement is 541 feet (165 meters), centered at 6788 feet (2069 meters) between the low elevation of 6037 feet and the high elevation of 8199 feet (1840 to 2499 meters).

10	11	
14	15	
17	18	19

ADJACENT PAGES

N

SCALE 1 INCH = ½ MILE

0 ½ 1 MILE

0 1000 2000 3000 4000 FEET

0 0.5 1 KILOMETER

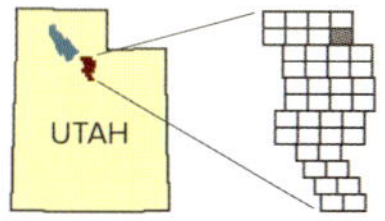

East Canyon

L R

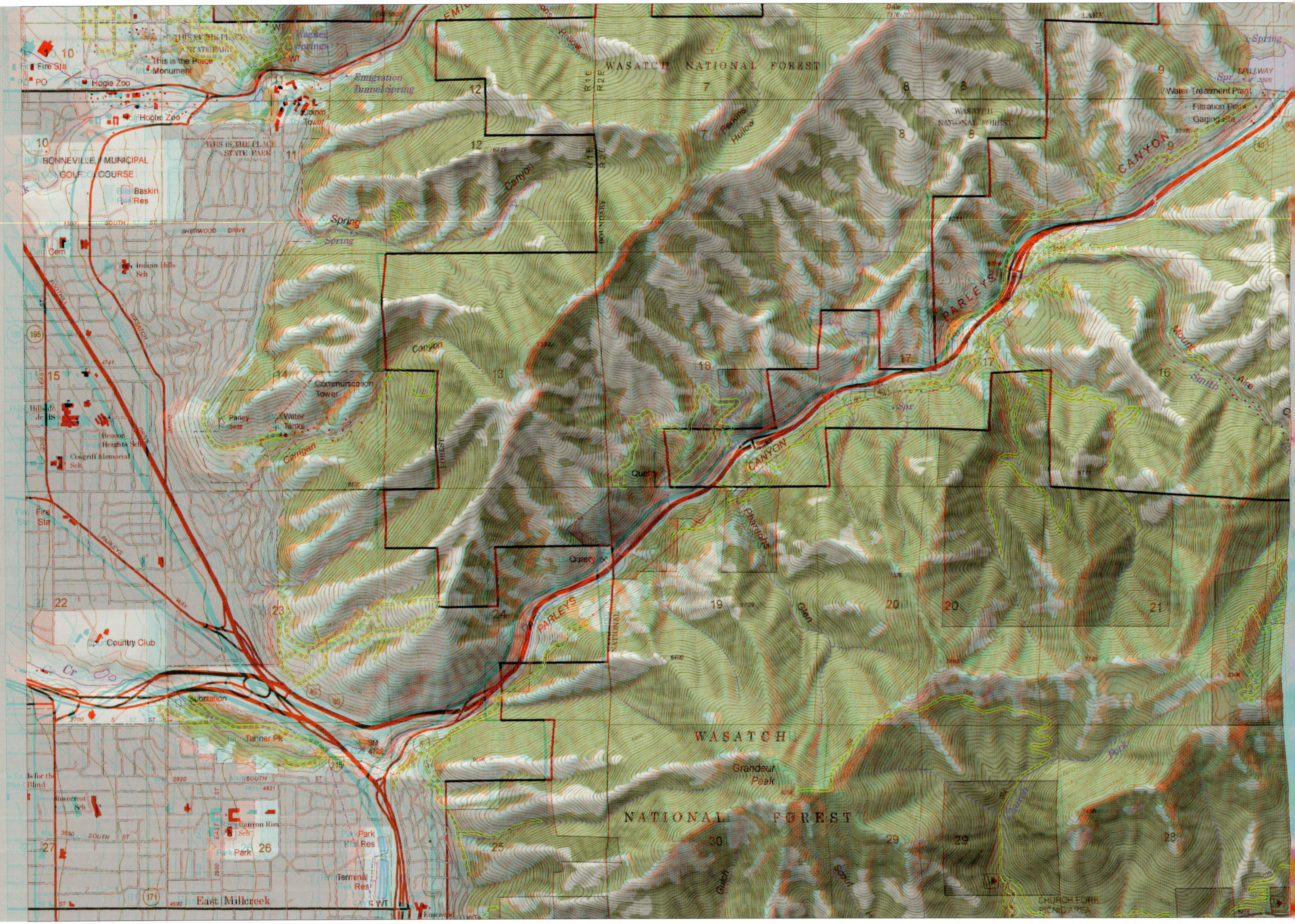

The anaglyph X displacement is 948 feet (289 meters), centered at 6529 feet (1990 meters) between the low elevation of 4518 feet and the high elevation of 8304 feet (1377 to 2531 meters).

12	13	14
	16	17
	20	21

ADJACENT PAGES

N

SCALE 1 INCH = ½ MILE

0 ½ 1 MILE

0 1000 2000 3000 4000 FEET

0 0.5 1 KILOMETER

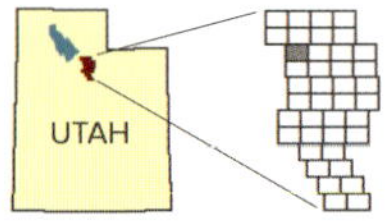

Parleys Canyon

L R

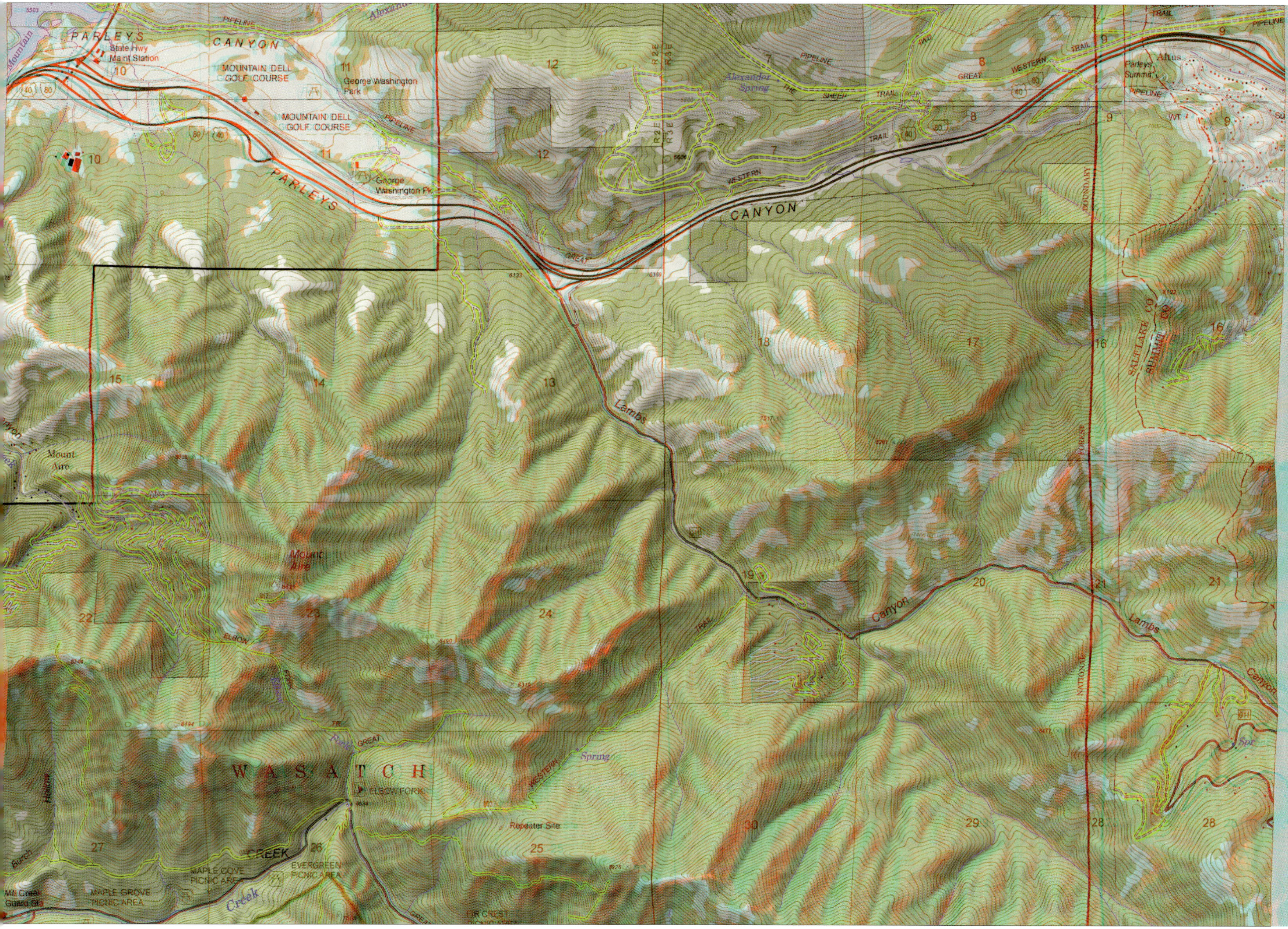

The anaglyph X displacement is 902 feet (275 meters), centered at 6529 feet (1990 meters) between the low elevation of 5396 feet and the high elevation of 9005 feet (1645 to 2745 meters).

13	14	15
16	17	18
20	21	22

ADJACENT PAGES

N

SCALE 1 INCH = ½ MILE

0 ½ 1 MILE

0 1000 2000 3000 4000 FEET

0 0.5 1 KILOMETER

UTAH

Lambs Canyon

L R

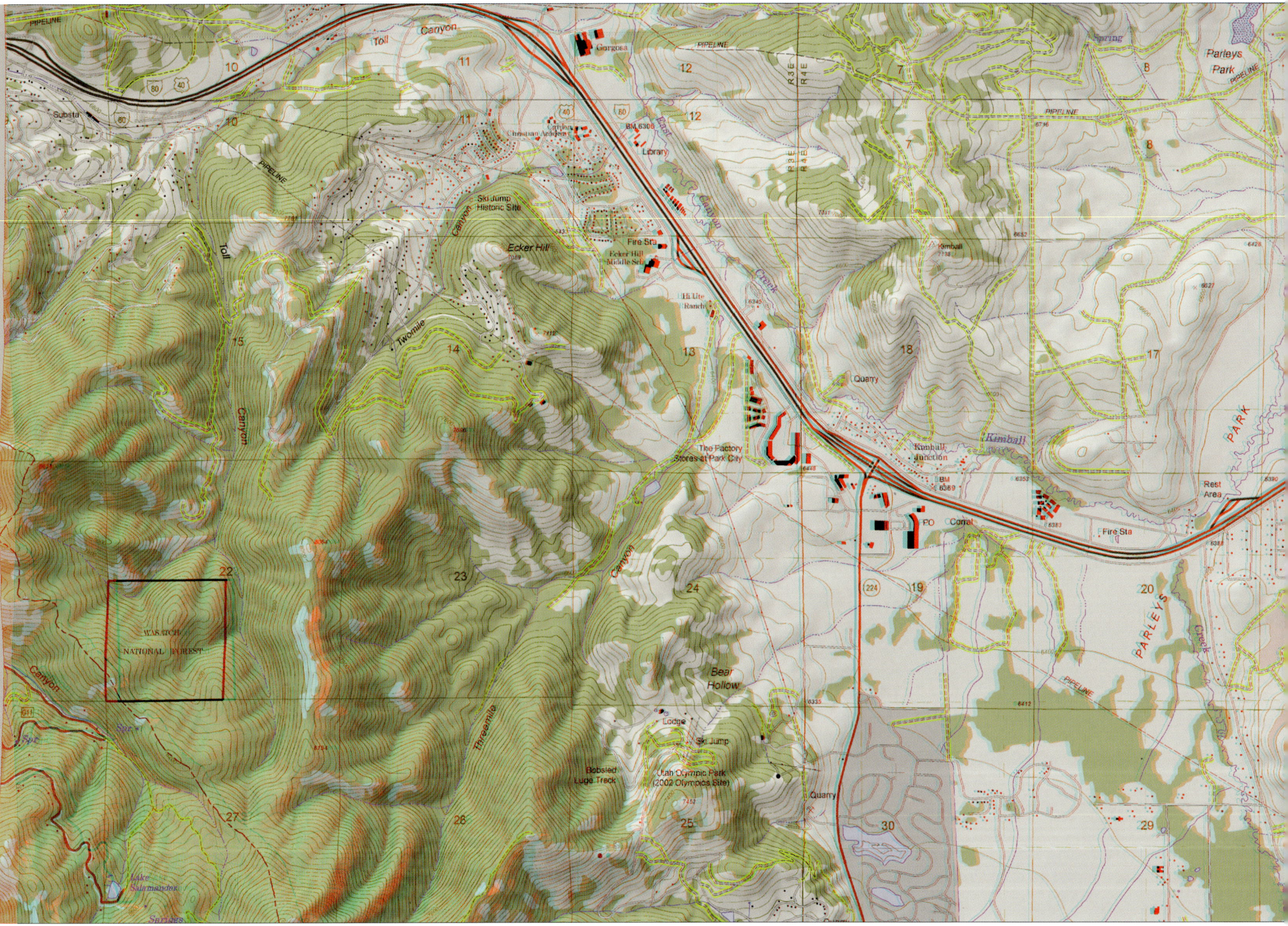

The anaglyph X displacement is 686 feet (209 meters), centered at 6834 feet (2083 meters) between the low elevation of 6272 feet and the high elevation of 9014 feet (1912 to 2748 meters).

14	15	
17	18	19
21	22	23

ADJACENT PAGES

N

SCALE 1 INCH = ½ MILE

0 ½ 1 MILE

0 1000 2000 3000 4000 FEET

0 0.5 1 KILOMETER

UTAH

Ecker Hill

L R

The anaglyph X displacement is 230 feet (70 meters), centered at 6834 feet (2083 meters) between the low elevation of 6334 feet and the high elevation of 7255 feet (1931 to 2211 meters).

	15	
	18	19
	22	23

ADJACENT PAGES

N

SCALE 1 INCH = ½ MILE

0 ½ 1 MILE

0 1000 2000 3000 4000 FEET

0 0.5 1 KILOMETER

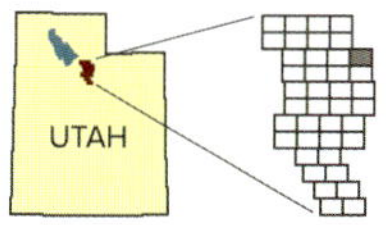

Silver Creek Junction

L R

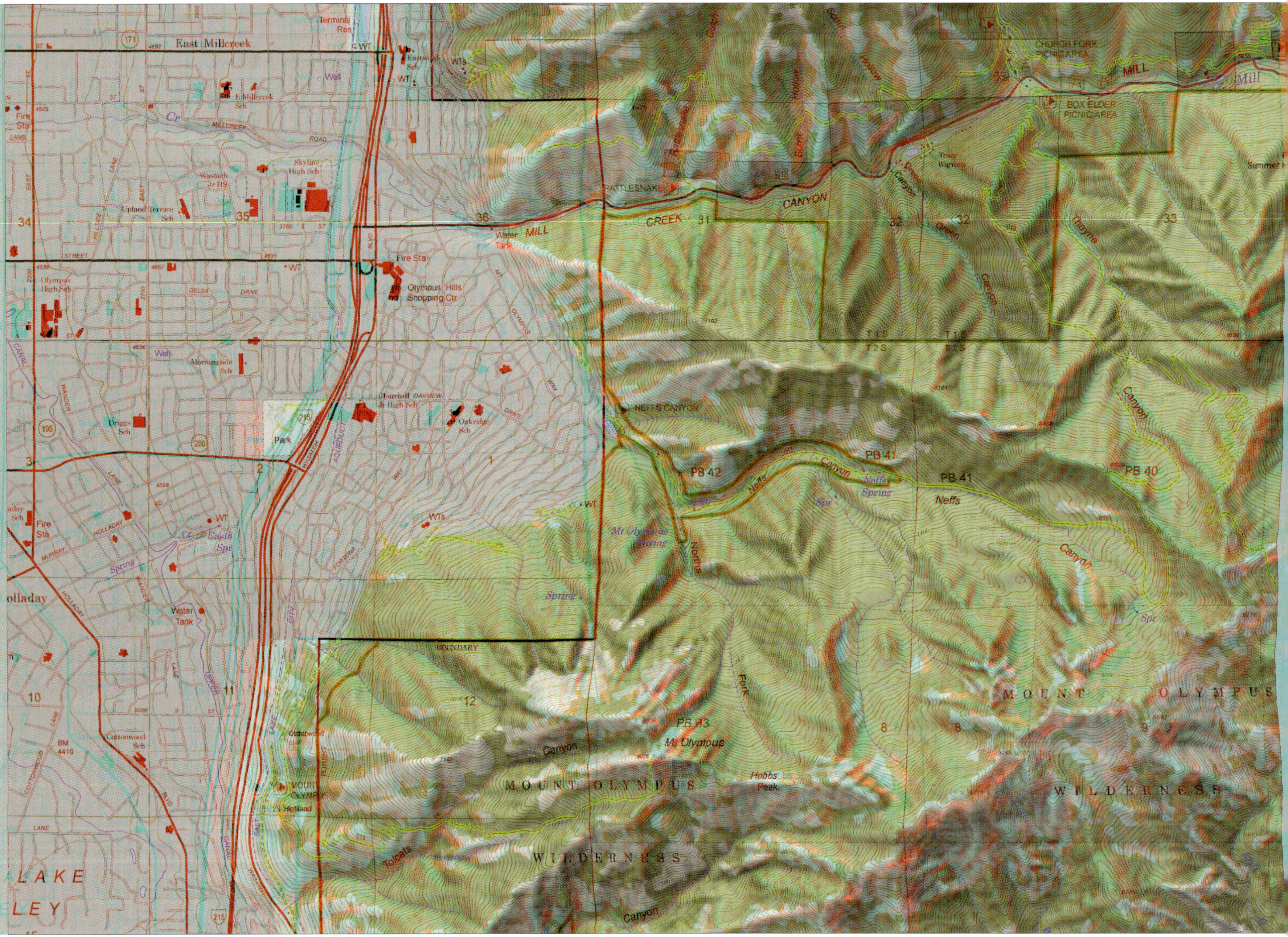

The anaglyph X displacement is 1342 feet (409 meters), centered at 7310 feet (2228 meters) between the low elevation of 4398 feet and the high elevation of 9766 feet (1340 to 2977 meters).

16	17
20	21
24	25

ADJACENT PAGES

N

SCALE 1 INCH = ½ MILE

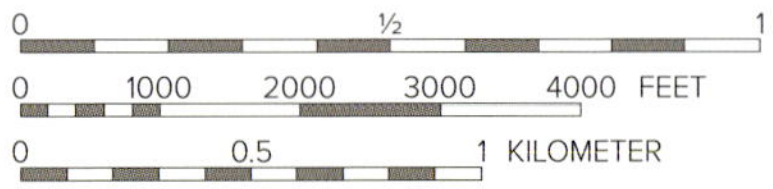

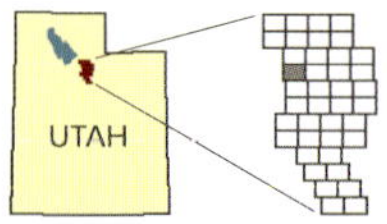

Mill Creek Canyon

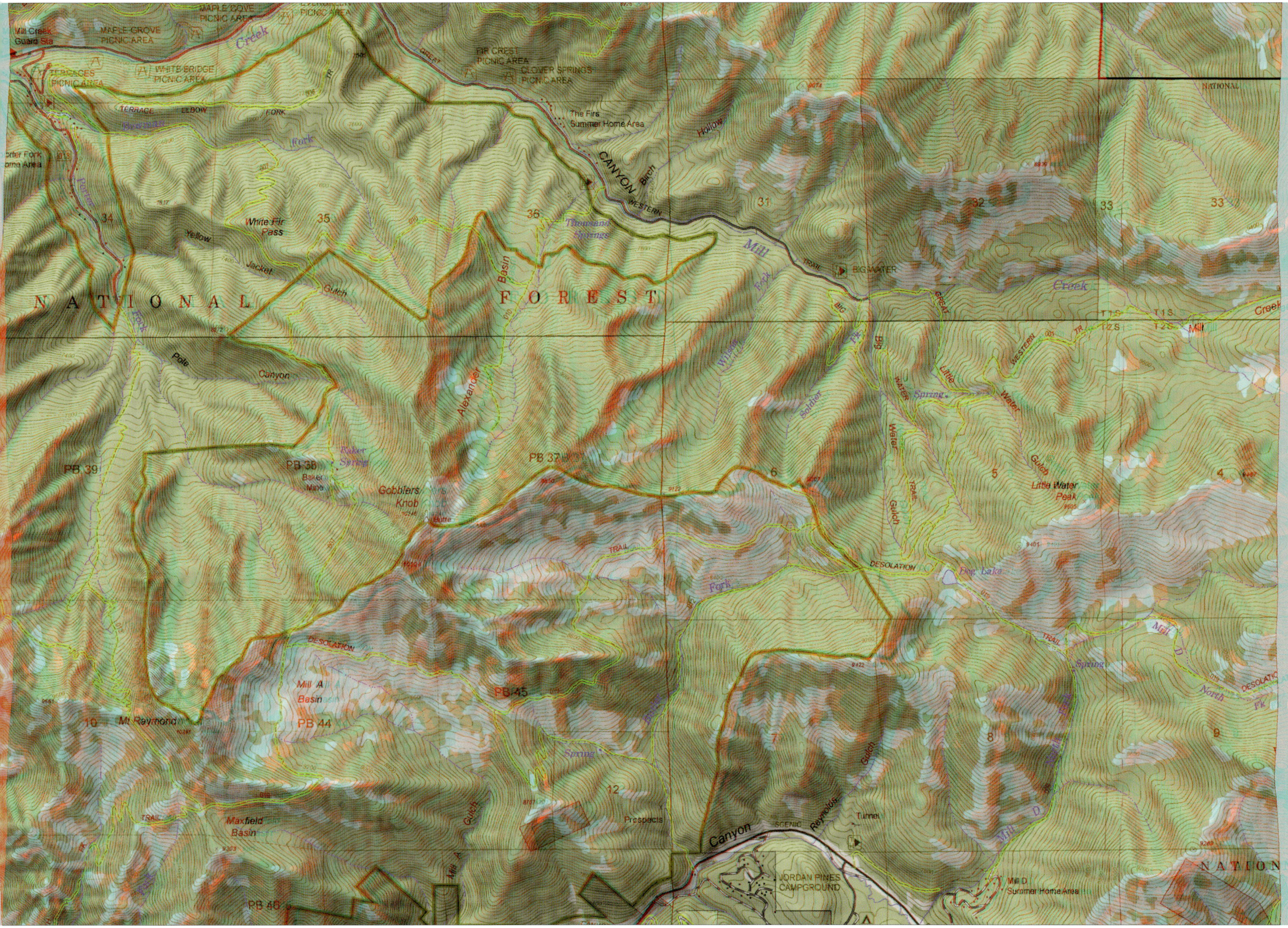

The anaglyph X displacement is 1070 feet (326 meters), centered at 7310 feet (2228 meters) between the low elevation of 5957 feet and the high elevation of 10241 feet (1816 to 3121 meters).

16	17	18
20	21	22
24	25	26

ADJACENT PAGES

N

SCALE 1 INCH = ½ MILE

0 ½ 1 MILE

0 1000 2000 3000 4000 FEET

0 0.5 1 KILOMETER

UTAH

Gobblers Knob

L R

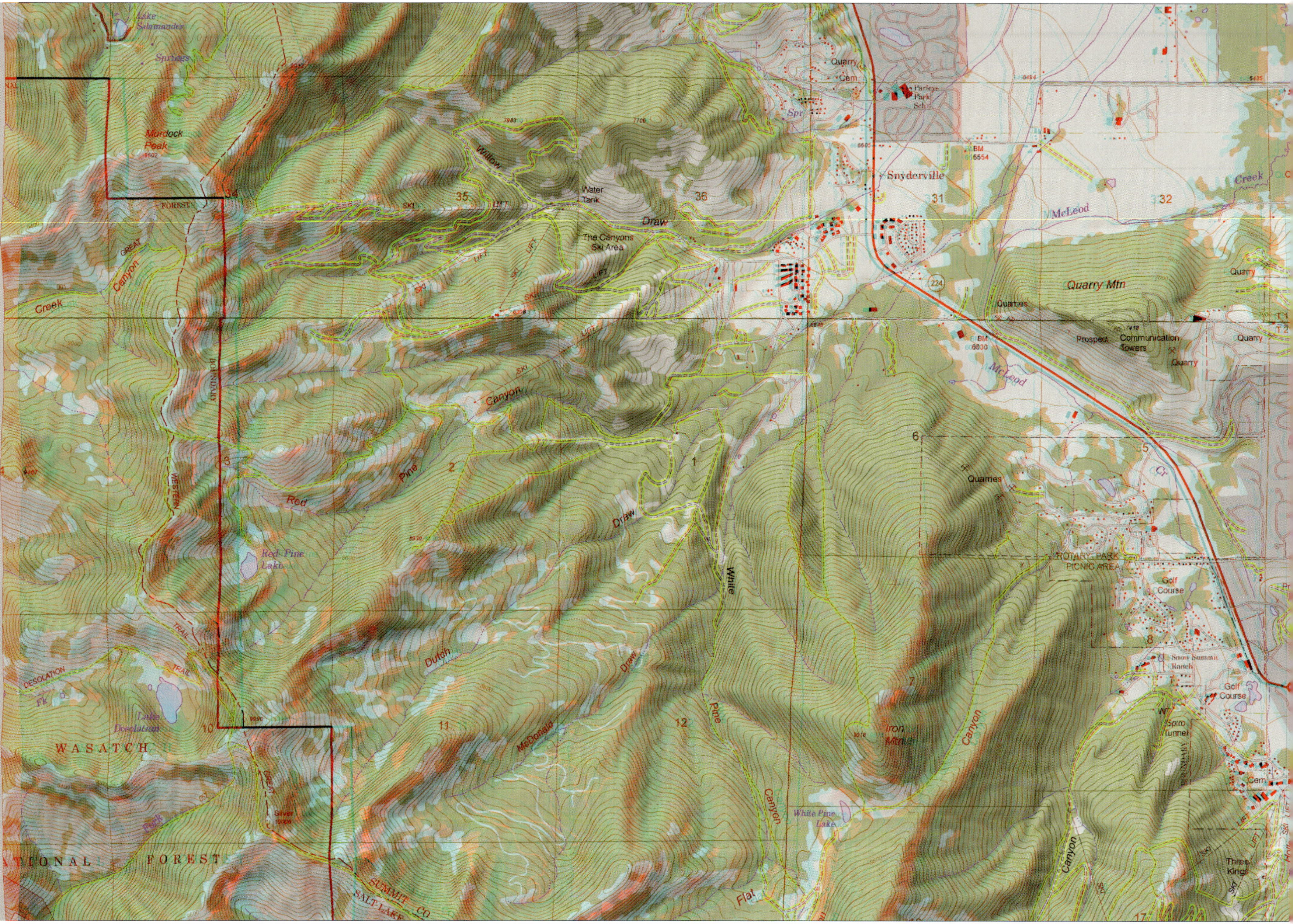

The anaglyph X displacement is 896 feet (273 meters), centered at 7444 feet (2269 meters) between the low elevation of 6434 feet and the high elevation of 10014 feet (1961 to 3052 meters).

17	18	19
21	22	23
25	26	27

ADJACENT PAGES

N

SCALE 1 INCH = ½ MILE

0 ½ 1 MILE

0 1000 2000 3000 4000 FEET

0 0.5 1 KILOMETER

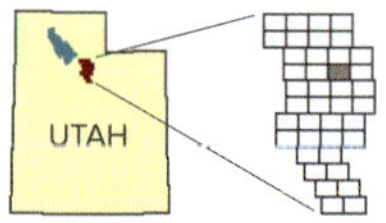

Murdock Peak

L R

The anaglyph X displacement is 417 feet (127 meters), centered at 7444 feet (2269 meters) between the low elevation of 6163 feet and the high elevation of 7835 feet (1879 to 2388 meters).

18	19
22	23
26	27

ADJACENT PAGES

N

SCALE 1 INCH = ½ MILE

0 ½ 1 MILE

0 1000 2000 3000 4000 FEET

0 0.5 1 KILOMETER

UTAH

Richardson Flat

L R

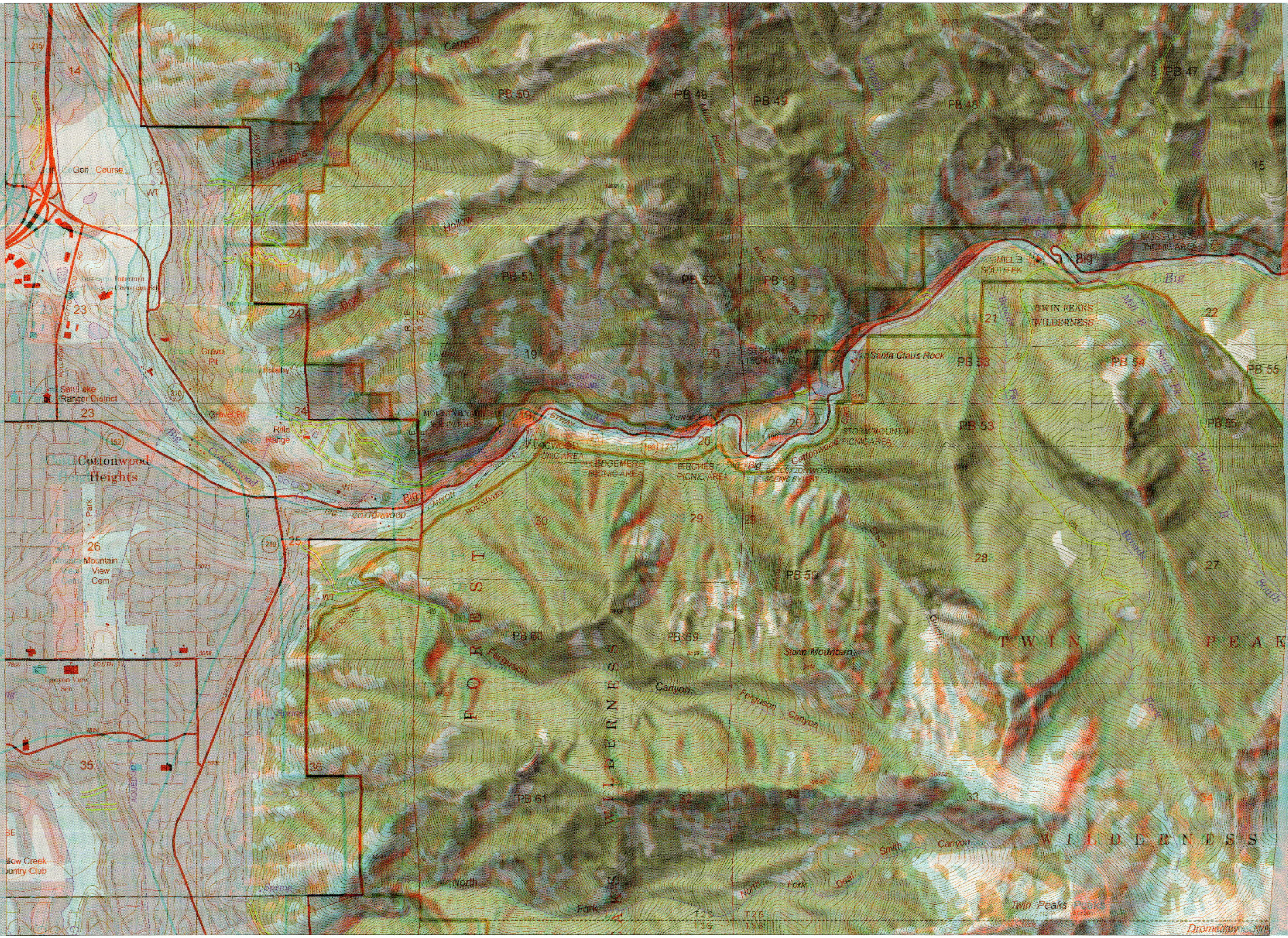

The anaglyph X displacement is 1719 feet (524 meters), centered at 7490 feet (2283 meters) between the low elevation of 4433 feet and the high elevation of 11305 feet (1351 to 3446 meters).

20	21
24	25
28	29

ADJACENT PAGES

N

SCALE 1 INCH = ½ MILE

0 ½ 1 MILE

0 1000 2000 3000 4000 FEET

0 0.5 1 KILOMETER

UTAH

Big Cottonwood Canyon

L R

The anaglyph X displacement is 1273 feet (388 meters), centered at 7490 feet (2283 meters) between the low elevation of 6236 feet and the high elevation of 11328 feet (1901 to 3453 meters).

20	21	22
24	25	26
28	29	30

ADJACENT PAGES

N

SCALE 1 INCH = ½ MILE

0 ½ 1 MILE

0 1000 2000 3000 4000 FEET

0 0.5 1 KILOMETER

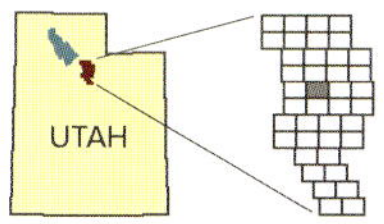

Kesler Peak

L R

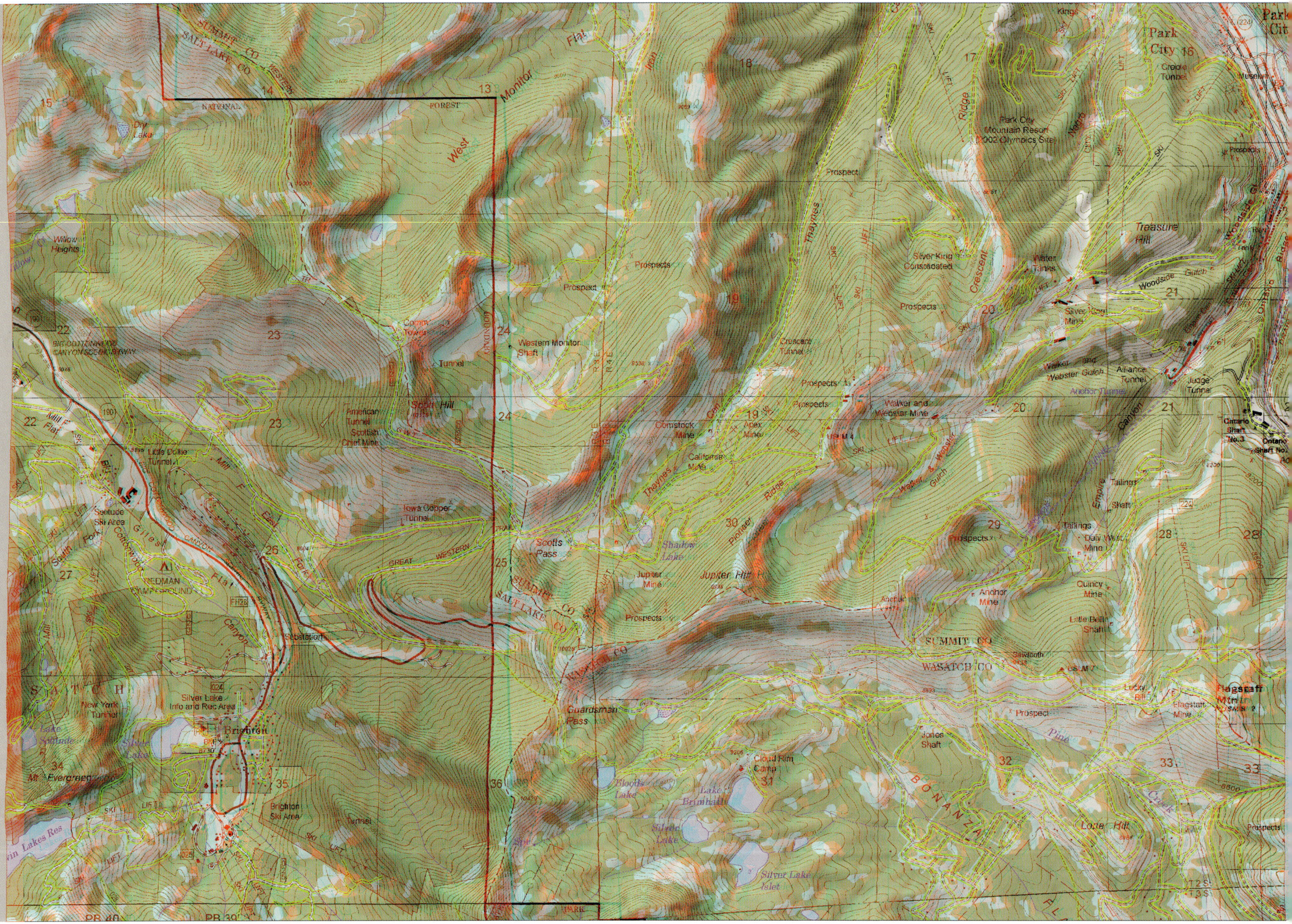

The anaglyph X displacement is 794 feet (242 meters), centered at 8173 feet (2491 meters) between the low elevation of 7376 feet and the high elevation of 10548 feet (2248 to 3215 meters).

21	22	23
25	26	27
29	30	31

ADJACENT PAGES

N

SCALE 1 INCH = ½ MILE

0 ½ 1 MILE

0 1000 2000 3000 4000 FEET

0 0.5 1 KILOMETER

UTAH

Guardsman Pass

L R

The anaglyph X displacement is 876 feet (267 meters), centered at 8173 feet (2491 meters) between the low elevation of 5861 feet and the high elevation of 9366 feet (1786 to 2855 meters).

22	23
26	27
30	31

ADJACENT PAGES

N

SCALE 1 INCH = ½ MILE

0 ½ 1 MILE

0 1000 2000 3000 4000 FEET

0 0.5 1 KILOMETER

UTAH

Flagstaff Mountain

L R

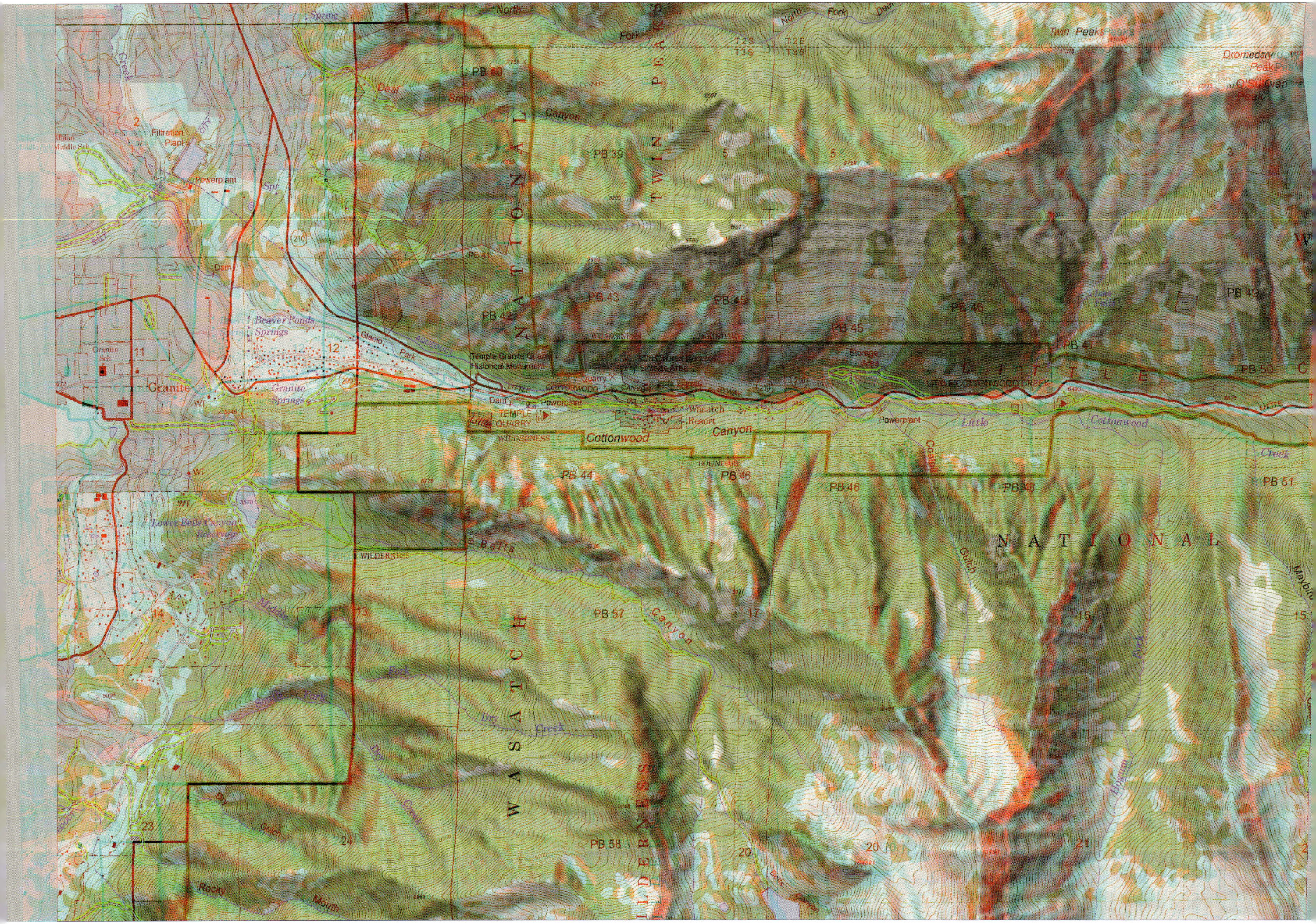

The anaglyph X displacement is 1650 feet (503 meters), centered at 8107 feet (2471 meters) between the low elevation of 4711 feet and the high elevation of 11307 feet (1436 to 3446 meters).

24	25
28	29
32	33

ADJACENT PAGES

N

SCALE 1 INCH = ½ MILE

0 ½ 1 MILE

0 1000 2000 3000 4000 FEET

0 0.5 1 KILOMETER

UTAH

Little Cottonwood Canyon

L R

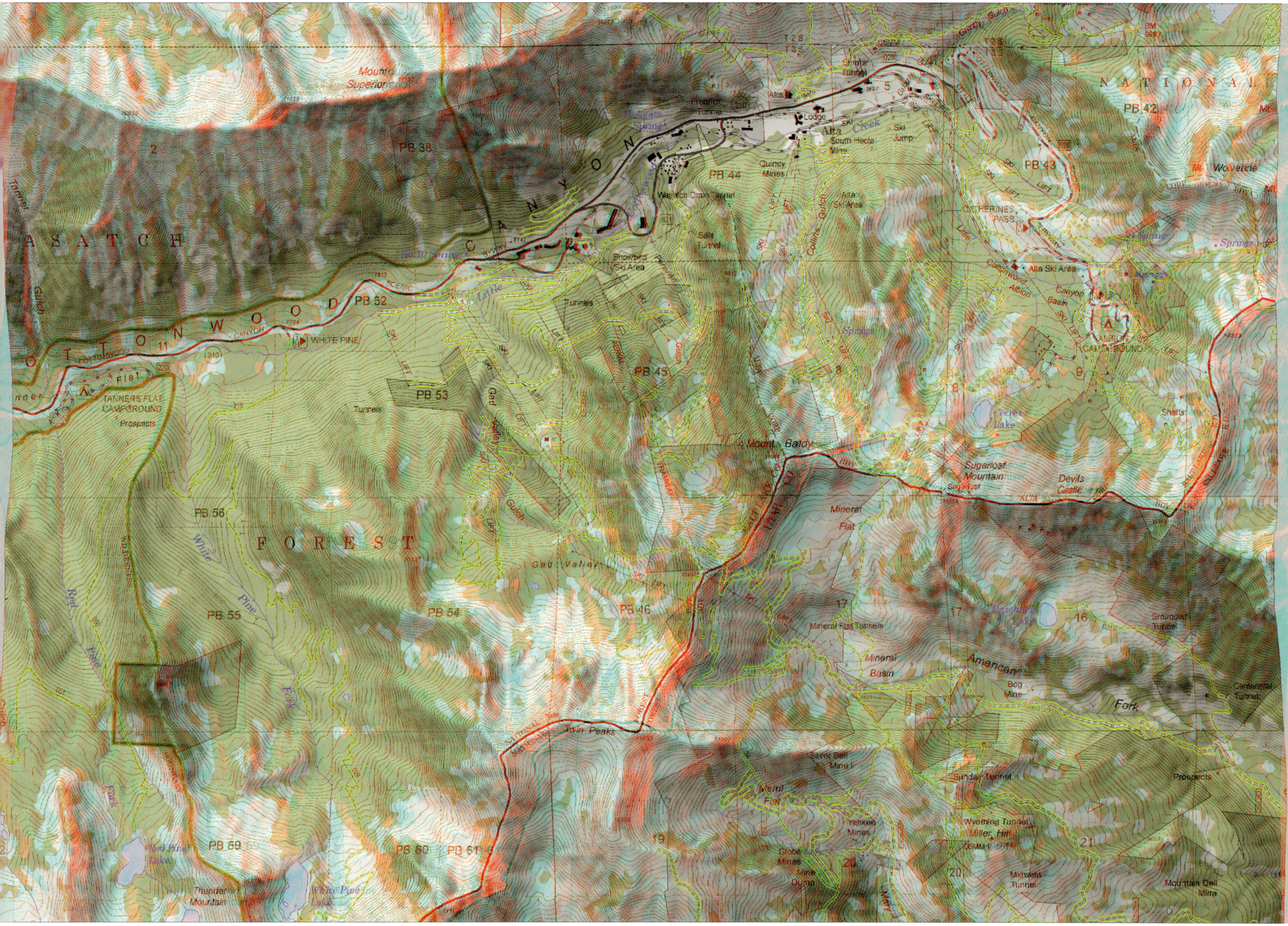

The anaglyph X displacement is 1250 feet (381 meters), centered at 8107 feet (2471 meters) between the low elevation of 6472 feet and the high elevation of 11466 feet (1973 to 3495 meters).

24	25	26
28	29	30
	33	34

ADJACENT PAGES

N

SCALE 1 INCH = ½ MILE

0 ½ 1 MILE

0 1000 2000 3000 4000 FEET

0 0.5 1 KILOMETER

UTAH

Albion Basin

L R

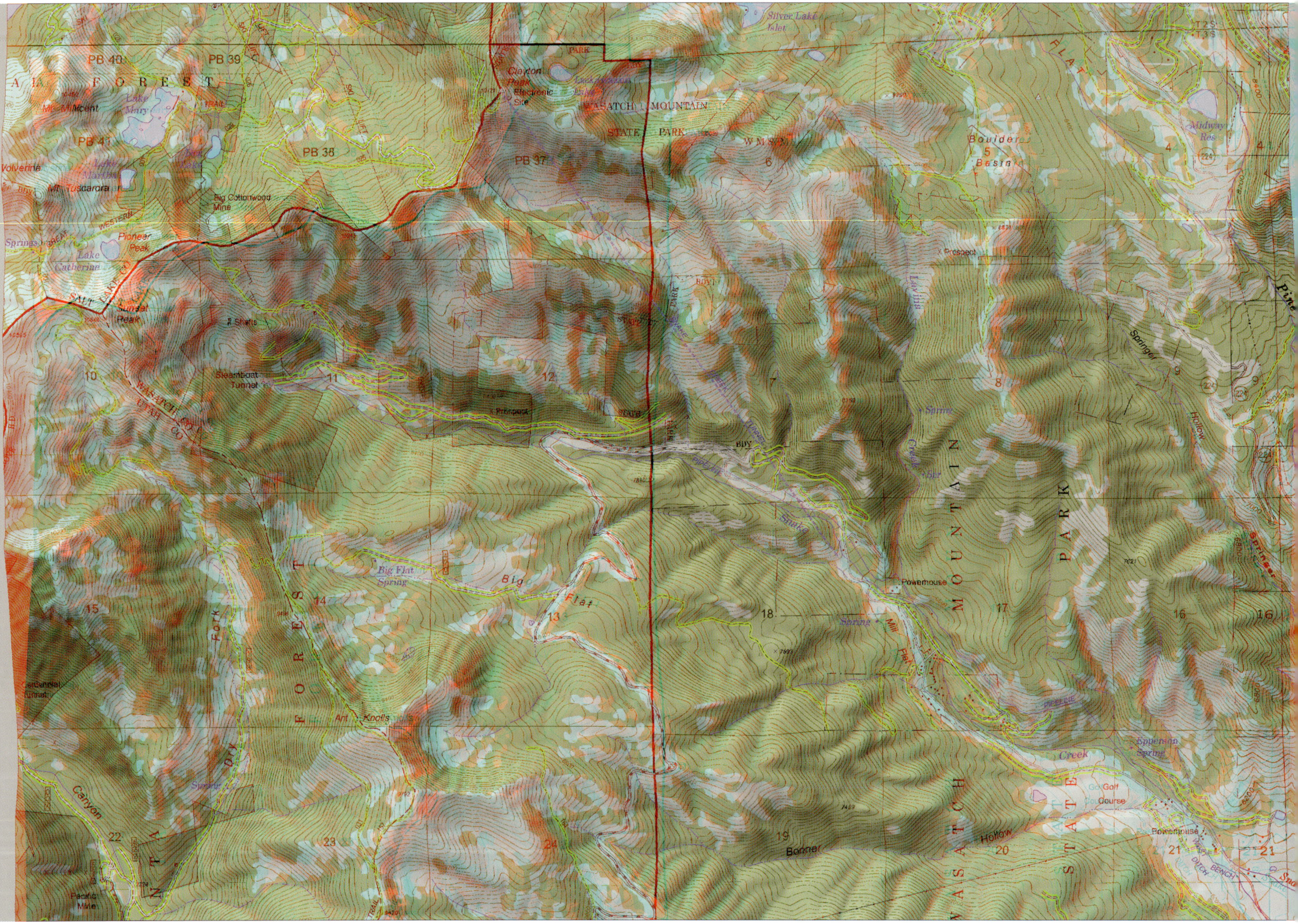

The anaglyph X displacement is 1152 feet (351 meters), centered at 7858 feet (2395 meters) between the low elevation of 6310 feet and the high elevation of 10913 feet (1923 to 3326 meters).

25	26	27
29	30	31
34	35	

ADJACENT PAGES

N

SCALE 1 INCH = ½ MILE

0 ½ 1 MILE

0 1000 2000 3000 4000 FEET

0 0.5 1 KILOMETER

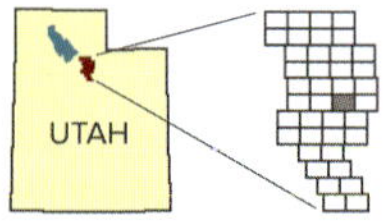

Lake Catherine

L R

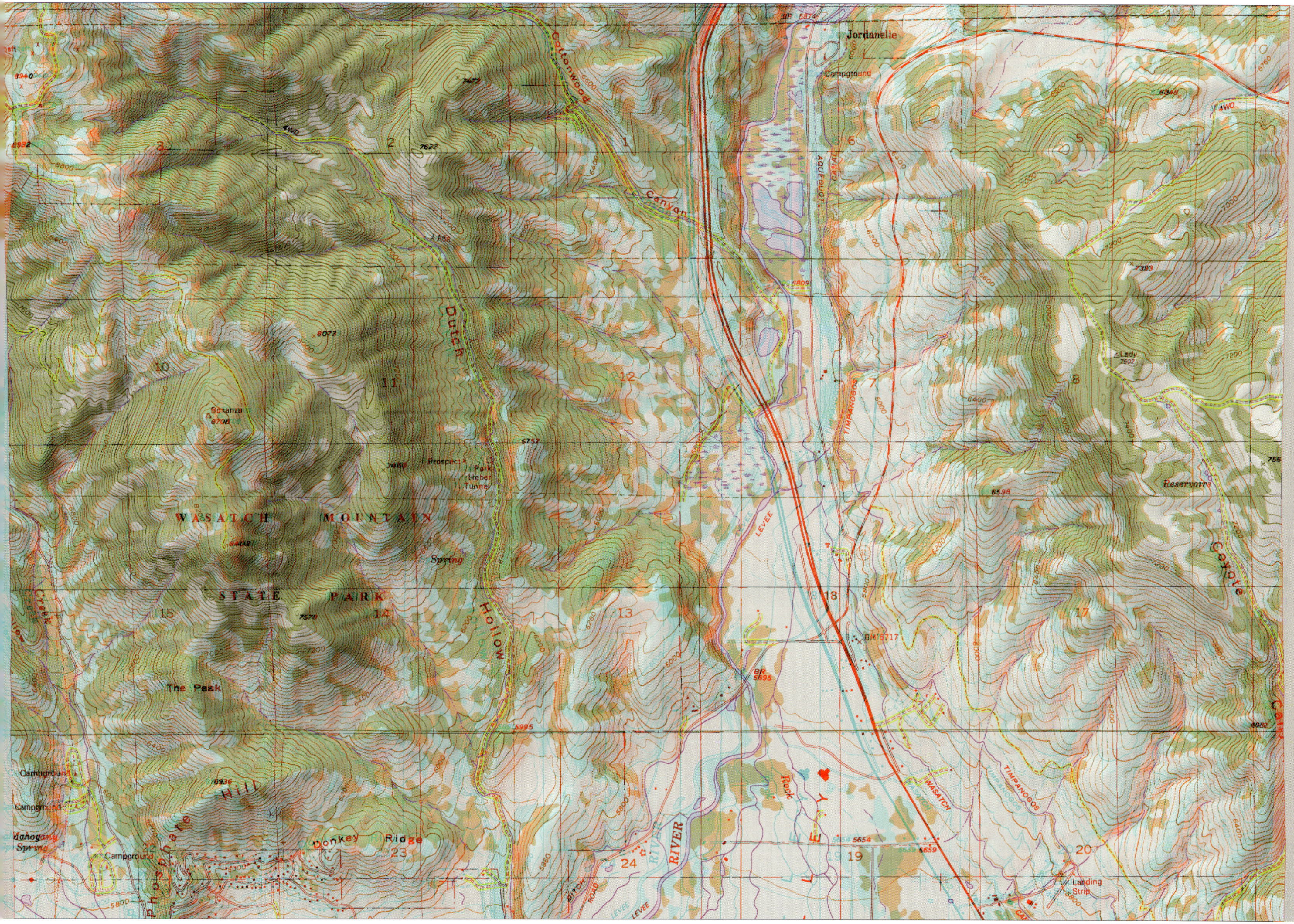

The anaglyph X displacement is 853 feet (260 meters), centered at 7858 feet (2395 meters) between the low elevation of 5619 feet and the high elevation of 9026 feet (1713 to 2751 meters).

26	27
30	31
35	

ADJACENT PAGES

N

SCALE 1 INCH = ½ MILE

0 ½ 1 MILE

0 1000 2000 3000 4000 FEET

0 0.5 1 KILOMETER

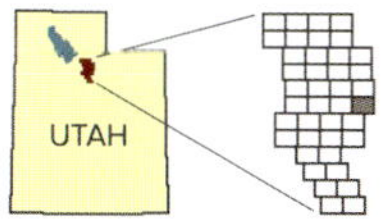

Phosphate Hill

L R

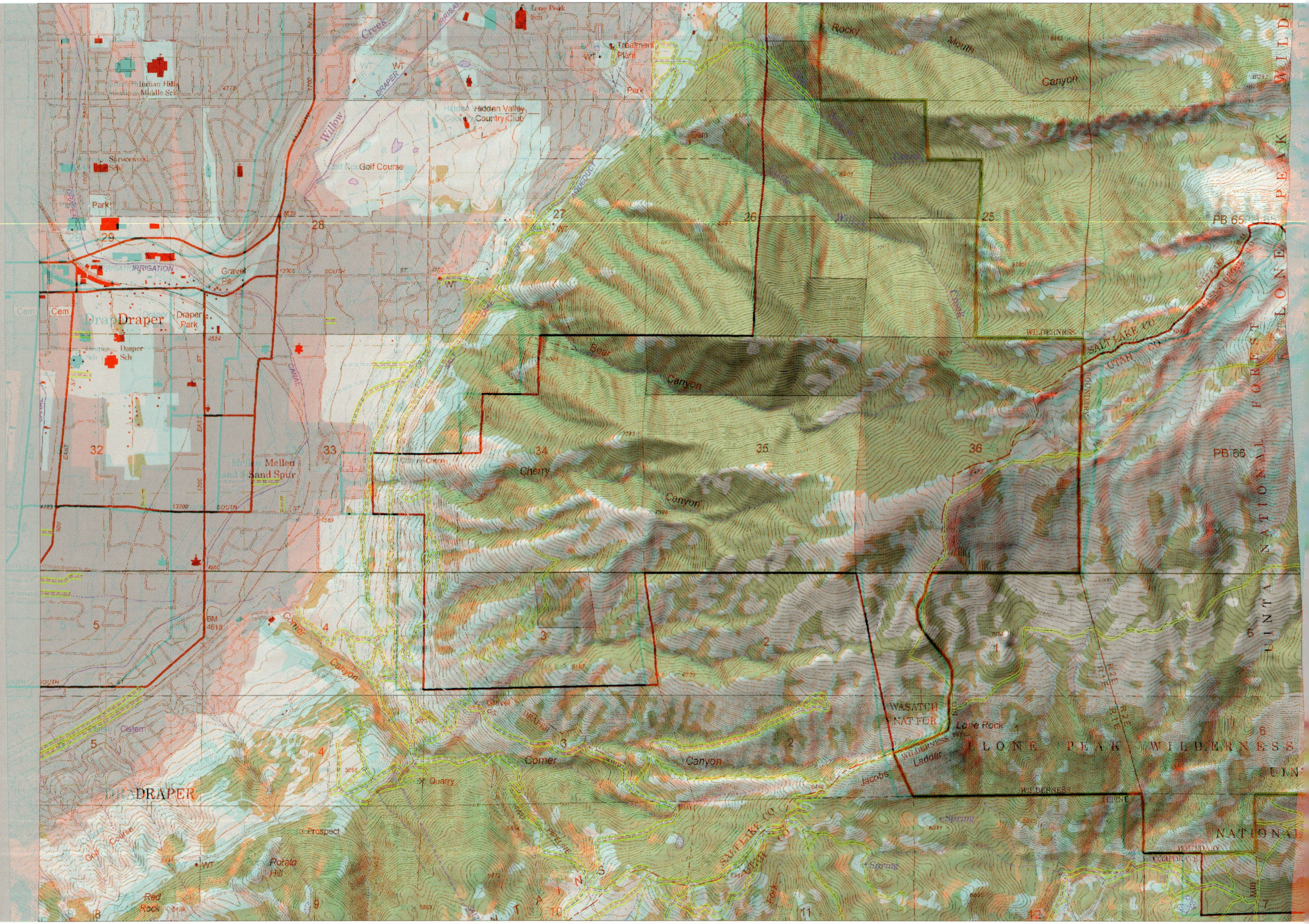

The anaglyph X displacement is 1680 feet (512 meters), centered at 7930 feet (2417 meters) between the low elevation of 4513 feet and the high elevation of 11232 feet (1376 to 3424 meters).

	28
32	33
36	37

ADJACENT PAGES

N

SCALE 1 INCH = ½ MILE

0 ½ 1 MILE

0 1000 2000 3000 4000 FEET

0 0.5 1 KILOMETER

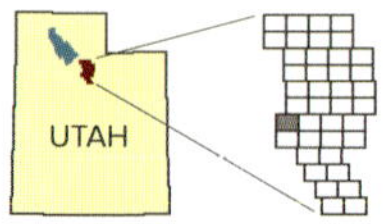

Jacobs Ladder

L R

The anaglyph X displacement is 1365 feet (416 meters), centered at 7930 feet (2417 meters) between the low elevation of 5850 feet and the high elevation of 11314 feet (1783 to 3449 meters).

	28	29
32	33	34
36	37	38

ADJACENT PAGES

N

SCALE 1 INCH = ½ MILE

0 ½ 1 MILE

0 1000 2000 3000 4000 FEET

0 0.5 1 KILOMETER

UTAH

The Pfeifferhorn

L R

The anaglyph X displacement is 1145 feet (349 meters), centered at 7408 feet (2258 meters) between the low elevation of 6419 feet and the high elevation of 10994 feet (1957 to 3351 meters).

	29	30
33	34	35
37	38	39

ADJACENT PAGES

N

SCALE 1 INCH = ½ MILE

0 ½ 1 MILE

0 1000 2000 3000 4000 FEET

0 0.5 1 KILOMETER

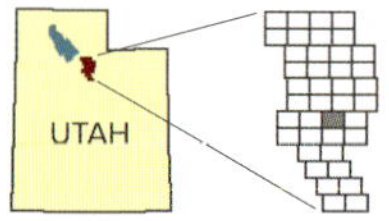

Graveyard Flat

L R

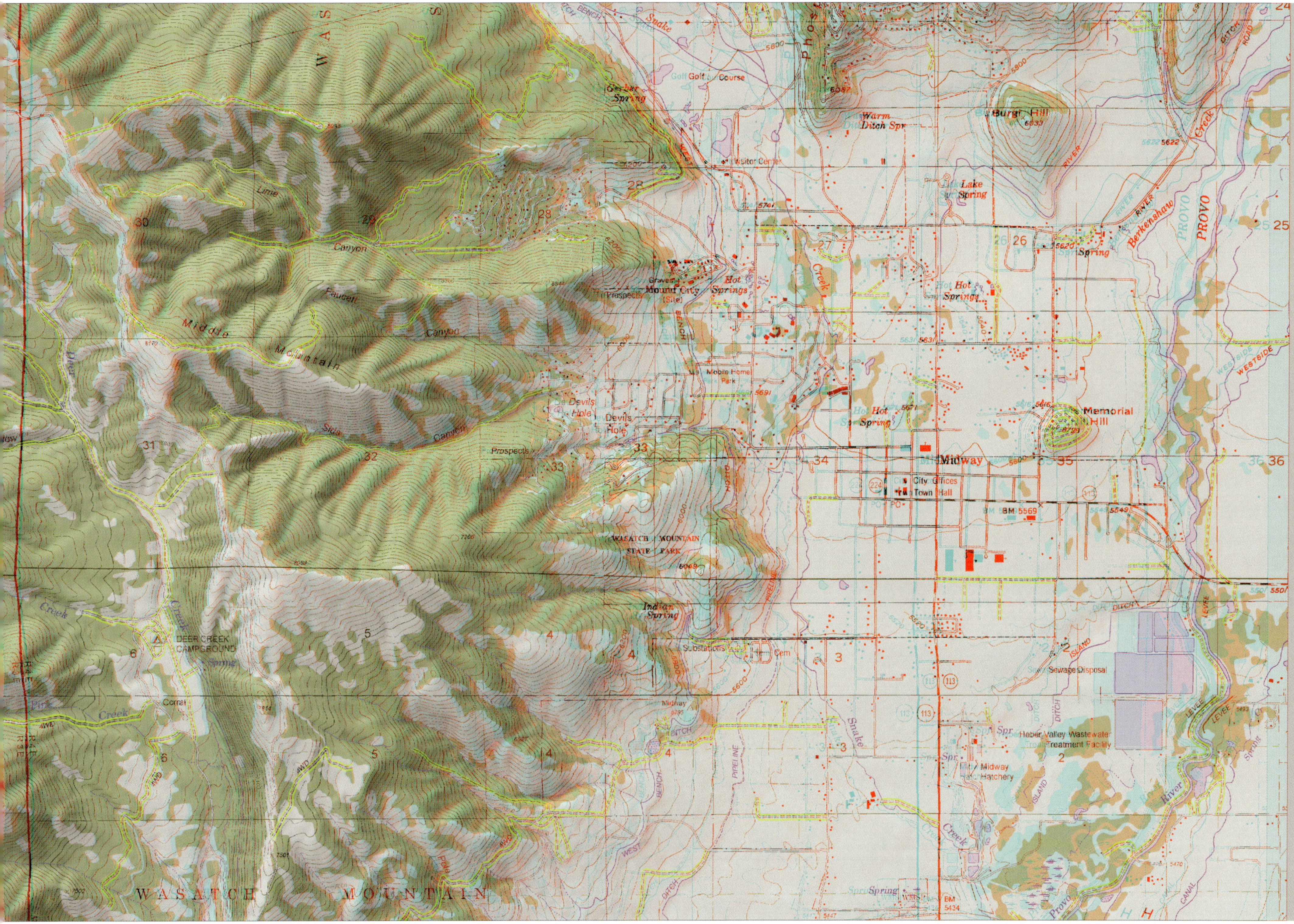

The anaglyph X displacement is 787 feet (240 meters), centered at 7408 feet (2258 meters) between the low elevation of 5440 feet and the high elevation of 8594 feet (1658 to 2619 meters).

29	30	31
34	35	
38	39	

ADJACENT PAGES

N

SCALE 1 INCH = ½ MILE

0 ½ 1 MILE

0 1000 2000 3000 4000 FEET

0 0.5 1 KILOMETER

UTAH

Memorial Hill

L R

The anaglyph X displacement is 479 feet (146 meters), centered at 6440 feet (1963 meters) between the low elevation of 4767 feet and the high elevation of 6687 feet (1453 to 2038 meters).

32	33
36	37
	40

ADJACENT PAGES

N

SCALE 1 INCH = ½ MILE

0 ½ 1 MILE

0 1000 2000 3000 4000 FEET

0 0.5 1 KILOMETER

UTAH

Traverse Mountains

L R

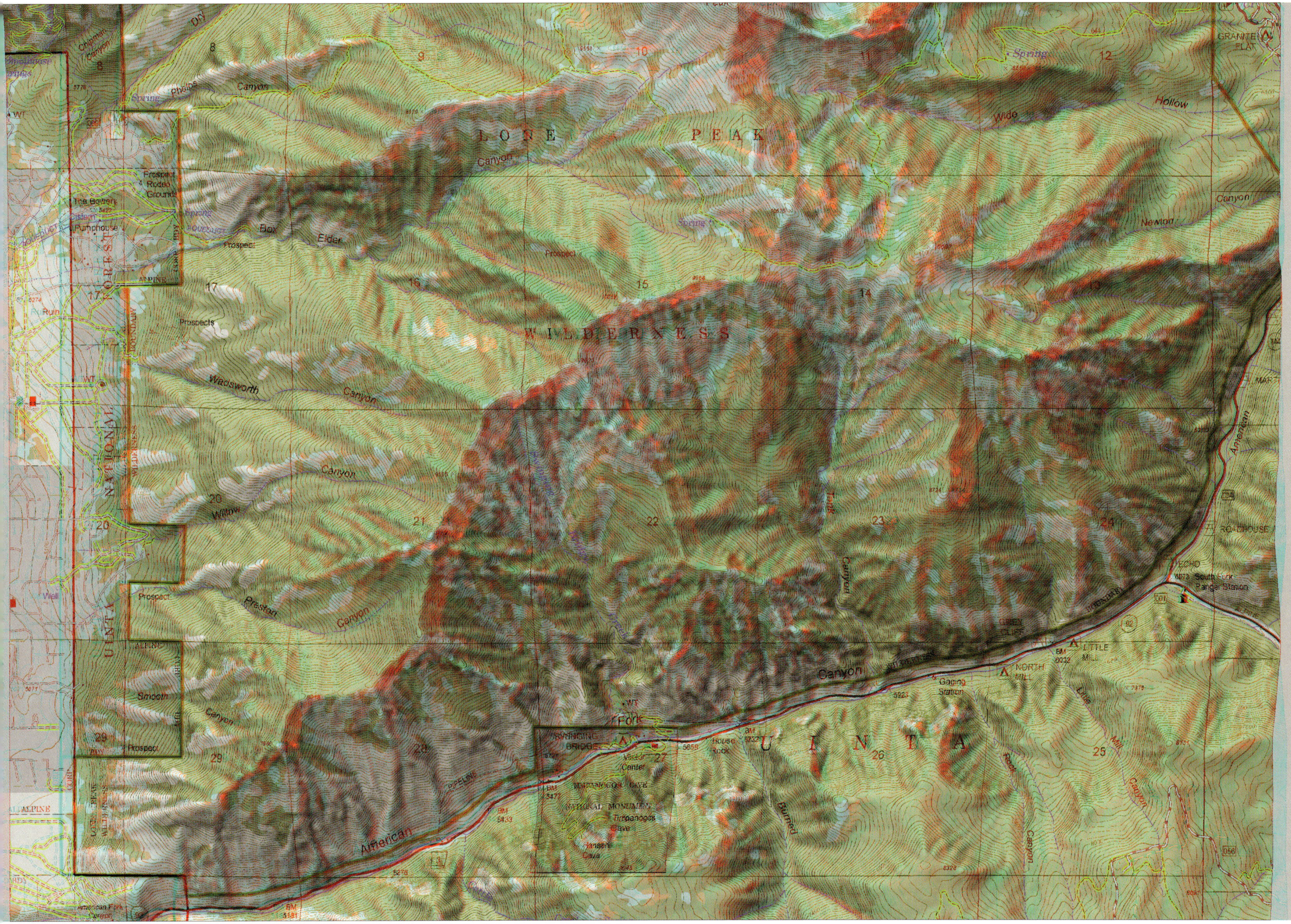

The anaglyph X displacement is 1509 feet (460 meters), centered at 6440 feet (1963 meters) between the low elevation of 5073 feet and the high elevation of 11105 feet (1546 to 3385 meters).

32	33	34
36	37	38
	40	41

ADJACENT PAGES

N

SCALE 1 INCH = ½ MILE

0 ½ 1 MILE

0 1000 2000 3000 4000 FEET

0 0.5 1 KILOMETER

UTAH

American Fork Canyon

L R

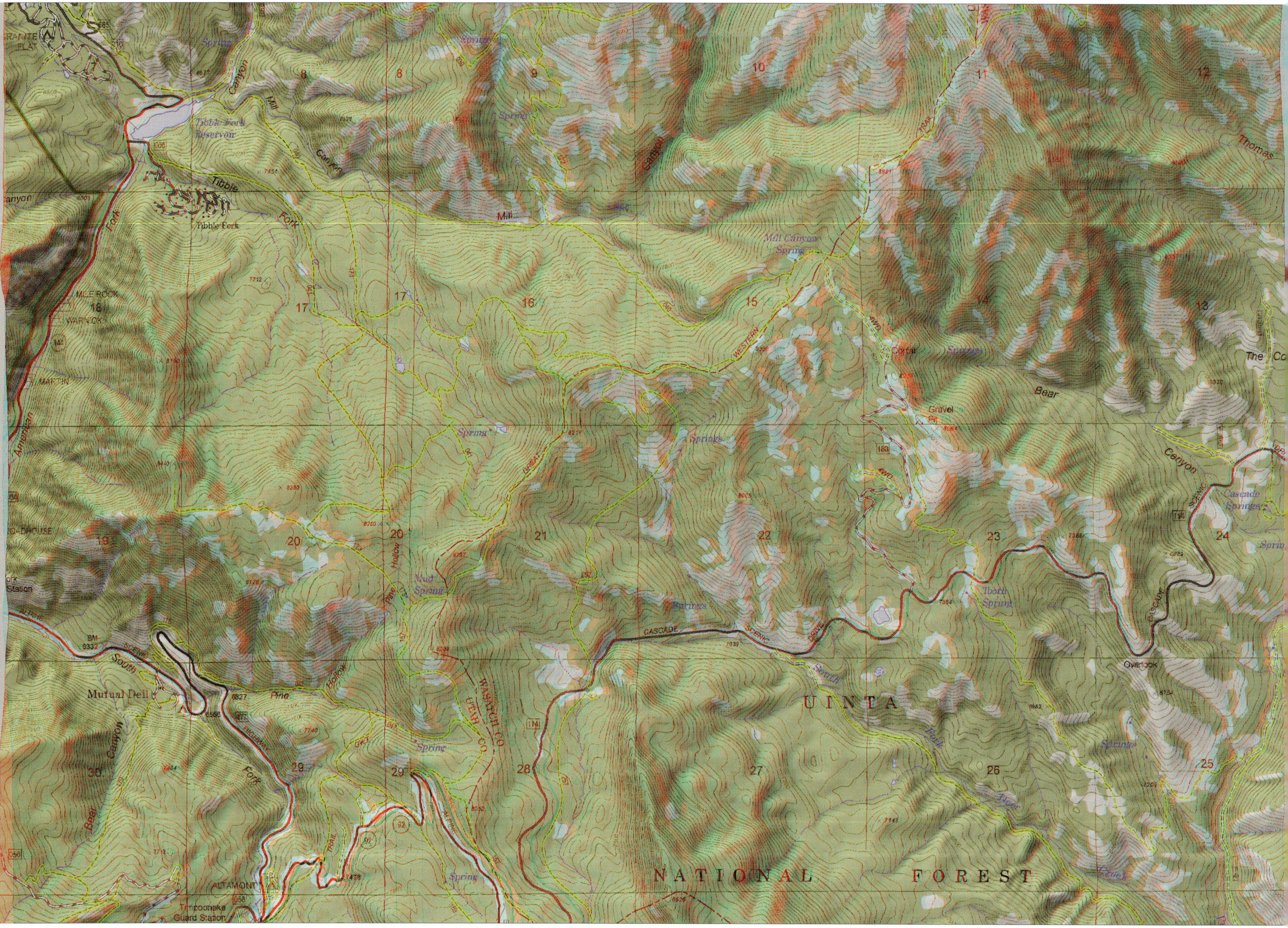

The anaglyph X displacement is 988 feet (301 meters), centered at 6742 feet (2055 meters) between the low elevation of 5852 feet and the high elevation of 9803 feet (1784 to 2988 meters).

33	34	35
37	38	39
40	41	

ADJACENT PAGES

N

SCALE 1 INCH = ½ MILE

0 ½ 1 MILE

0 1000 2000 3000 4000 FEET

0 0.5 1 KILOMETER

UTAH

Bear Canyon

L R

The anaglyph X displacement is 600 feet (183 meters), centered at 6742 feet (2055 meters) between the low elevation of 5421 feet and the high elevation of 7825 feet (1652 to 2385 meters).

34	35
38	39
41	

ADJACENT PAGES

N

SCALE 1 INCH = ½ MILE

0 ½ 1 MILE

0 1000 2000 3000 4000 FEET

0 0.5 1 KILOMETER

UTAH

Soldier Hollow

L R

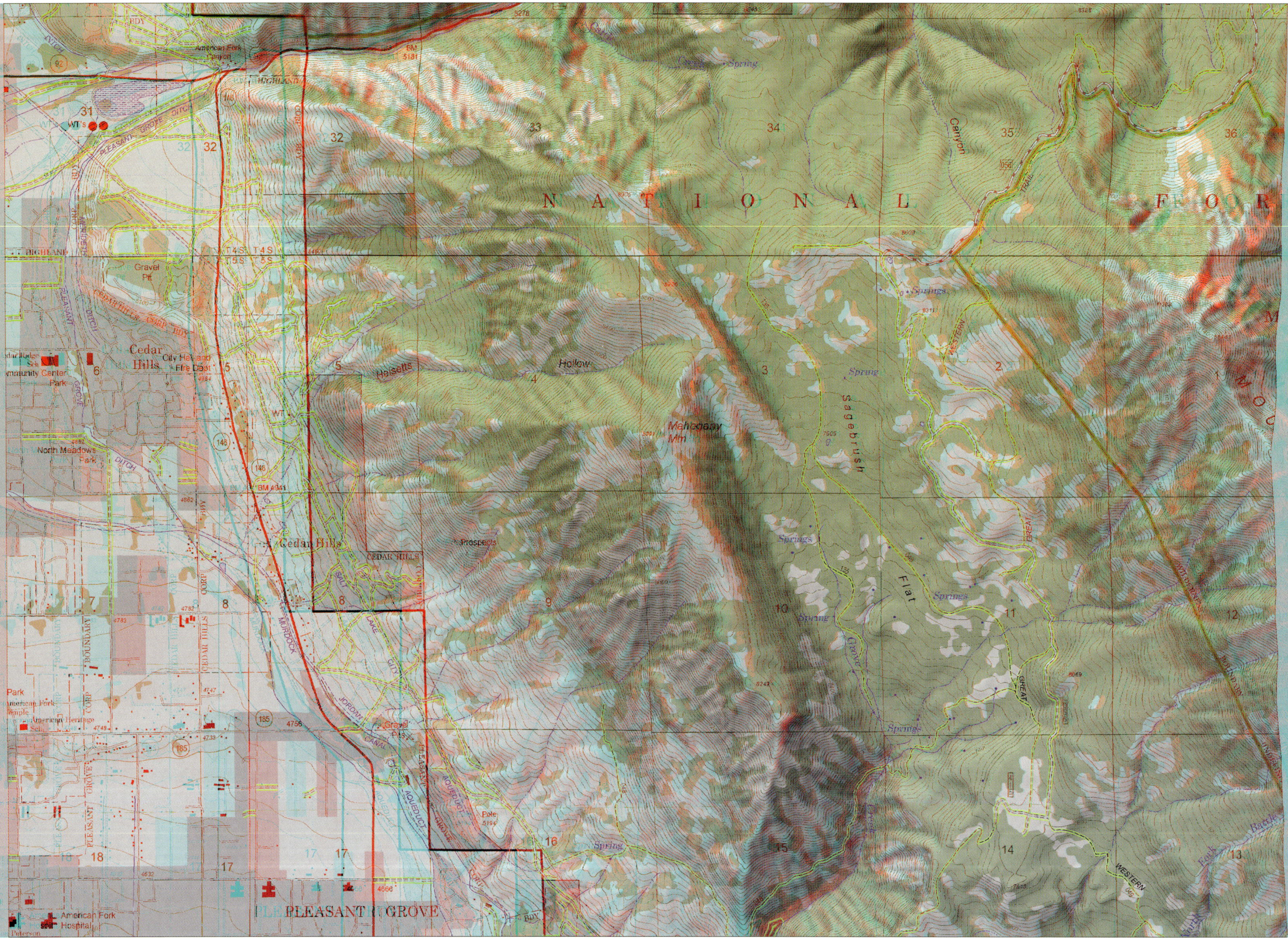

The anaglyph X displacement is 1709 feet (521 meters), centered at 7533 feet (2296 meters) between the low elevation of 4597 feet and the high elevation of 11433 feet (1401 to 3485 meters).

36	37	38
	40	41
	42	43

ADJACENT PAGES

SCALE 1 INCH = ½ MILE

0 ½ 1 MILE

0 1000 2000 3000 4000 FEET

0 0.5 1 KILOMETER

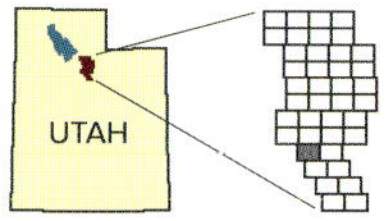

Mahogany Mountain

L R

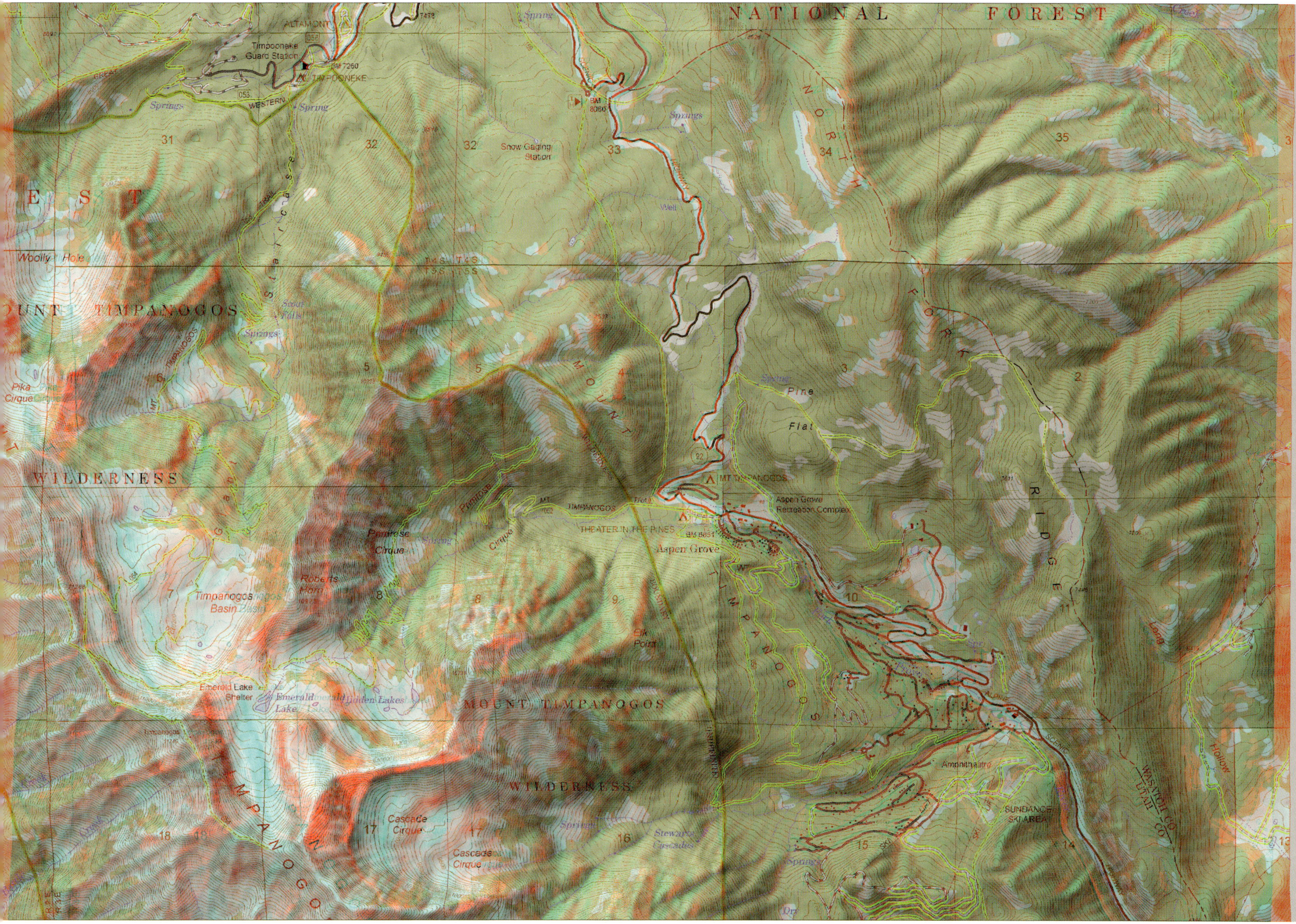

The anaglyph X displacement is 1509 feet (460 meters), centered at 7533 feet (2296 meters) between the low elevation of 5697 feet and the high elevation of 11739 feet (1736 to 3578 meters).

37	38	39
40	41	
42	43	

ADJACENT PAGES

N

SCALE 1 INCH = ½ MILE

0 ½ 1 MILE

0 1000 2000 3000 4000 FEET

0 0.5 1 KILOMETER

UTAH

Mount Timpanogos

L R

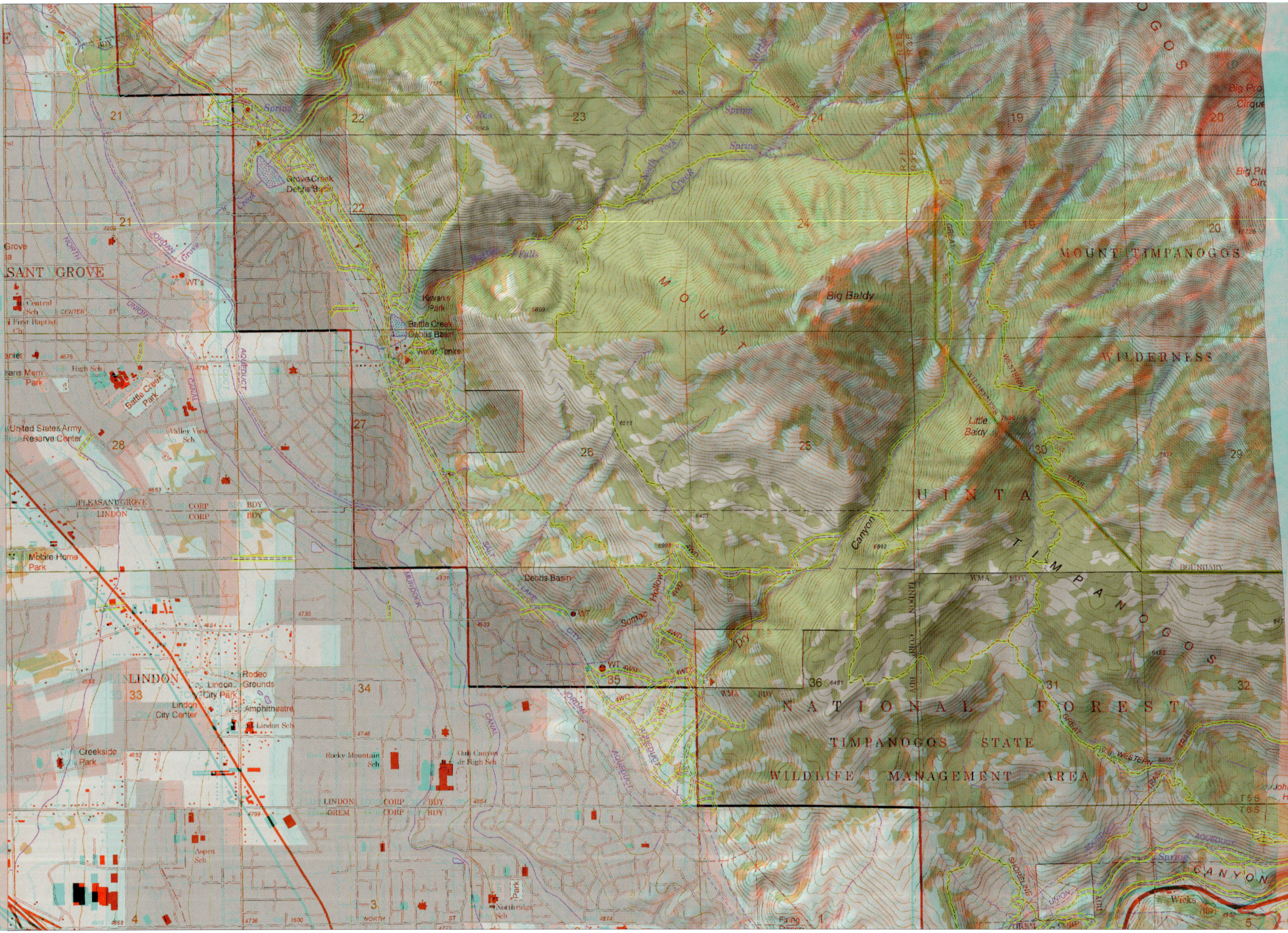

The anaglyph X displacement is 1759 feet (536 meters), centered at 6486 feet (1977 meters) between the low elevation of 4552 feet and the high elevation of 11586 feet (1388 to 3531 meters).

40	41
42	43
44	45

ADJACENT PAGES

N

SCALE 1 INCH = ½ MILE

0 ½ 1 MILE

0 1000 2000 3000 4000 FEET

0 0.5 1 KILOMETER

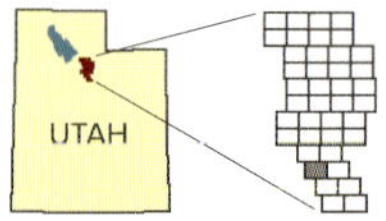

Big Baldy

L R

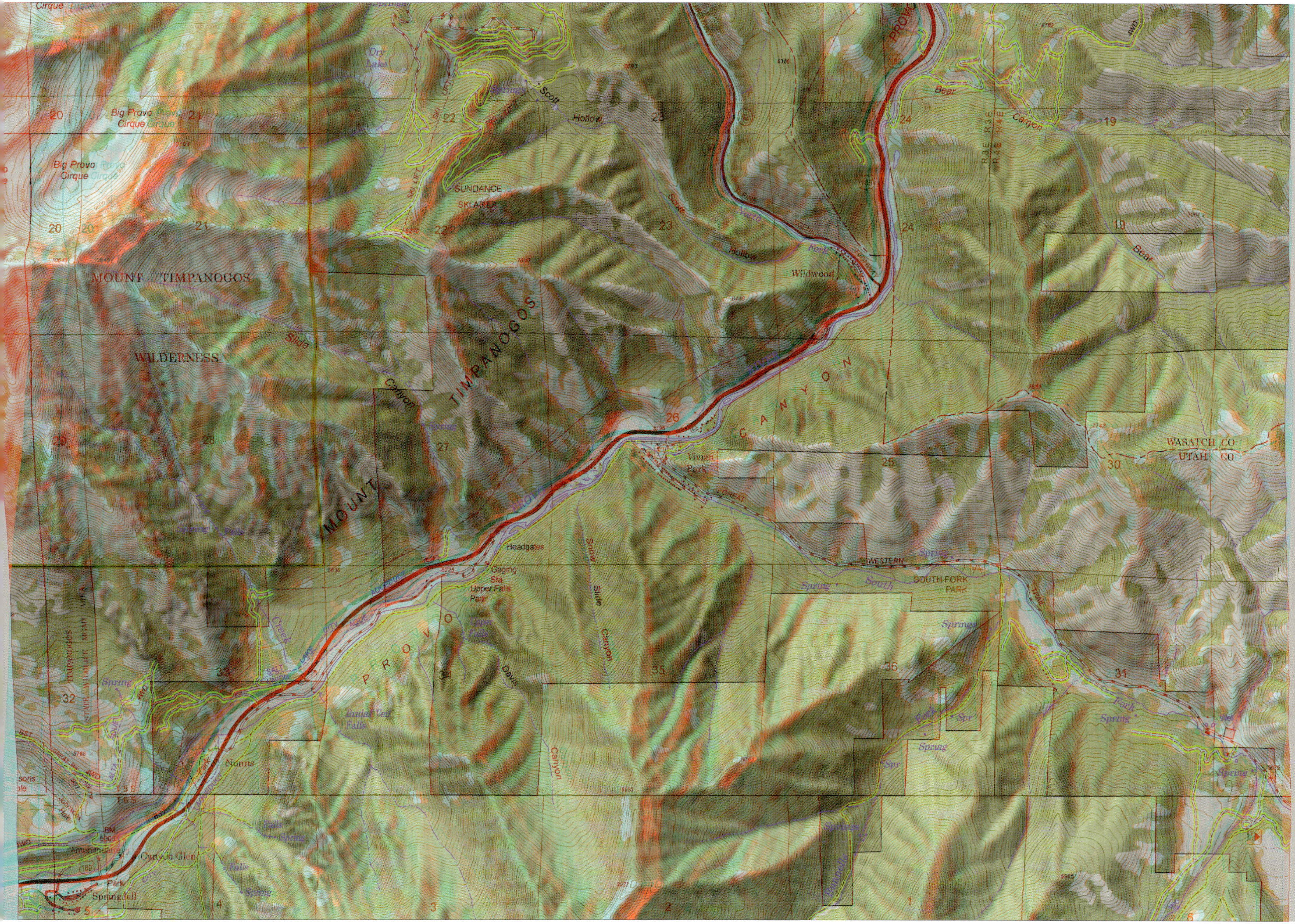

The anaglyph X displacement is 1621 feet (494 meters), centered at 6486 feet (1977 meters) between the low elevation of 4948 feet and the high elevation of 11425 feet (1508 to 3482 meters).

40	41
42	43
44	45

ADJACENT PAGES

N

SCALE 1 INCH = ½ MILE

0 ½ 1 MILE

0 1000 2000 3000 4000 FEET

0 0.5 1 KILOMETER

UTAH

Vivian Park

L R

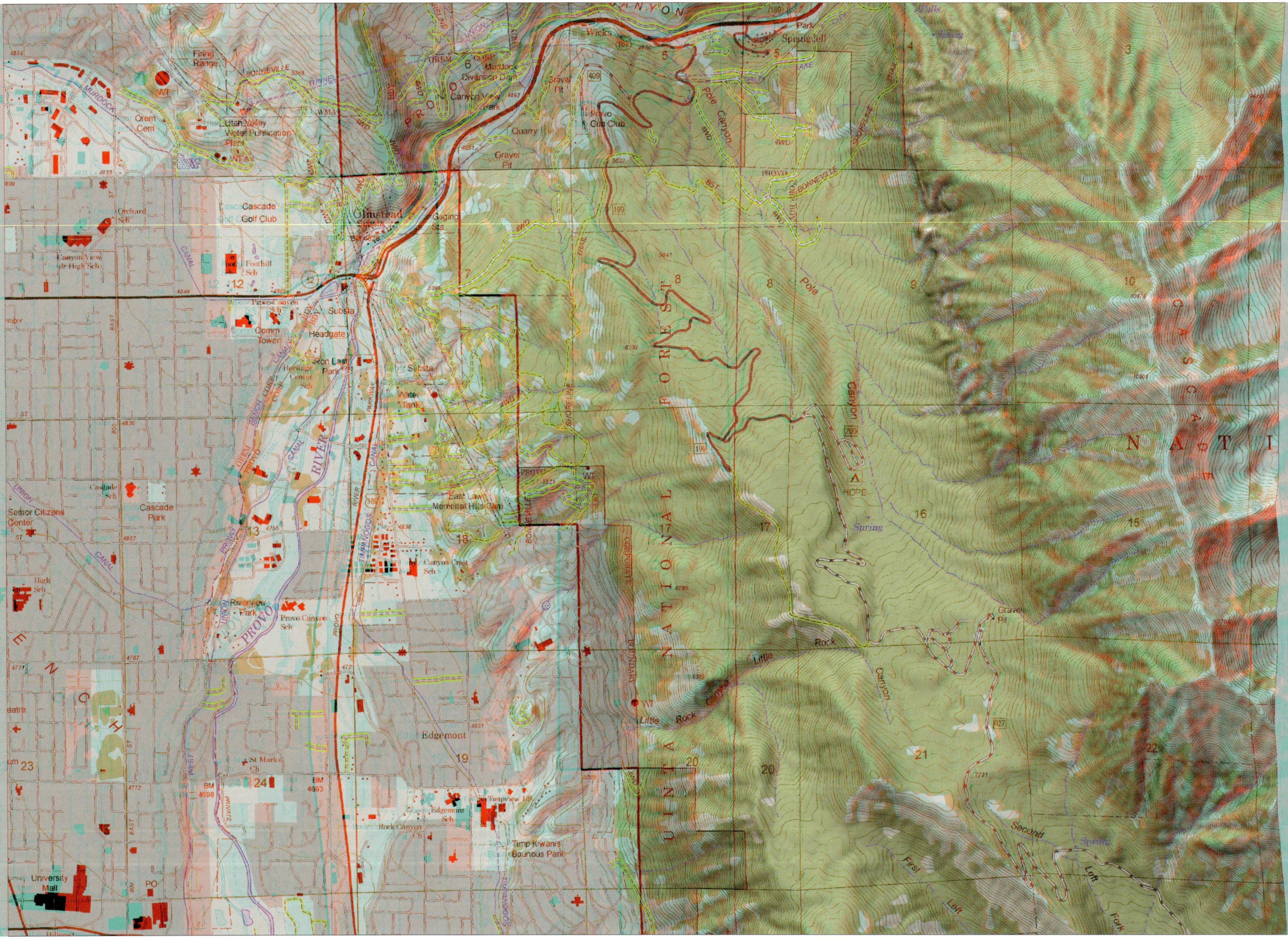

The anaglyph X displacement is 1562 feet (476 meters), centered at 7096 feet (2163 meters) between the low elevation of 4653 feet and the high elevation of 10894 feet (1418 to 3321 meters).

42	43	
	44	45
	46	47

ADJACENT PAGES

N

SCALE 1 INCH = ½ MILE

0 ½ 1 MILE

0 1000 2000 3000 4000 FEET

0 0.5 1 KILOMETER

UTAH

Little Rock Canyon

L R

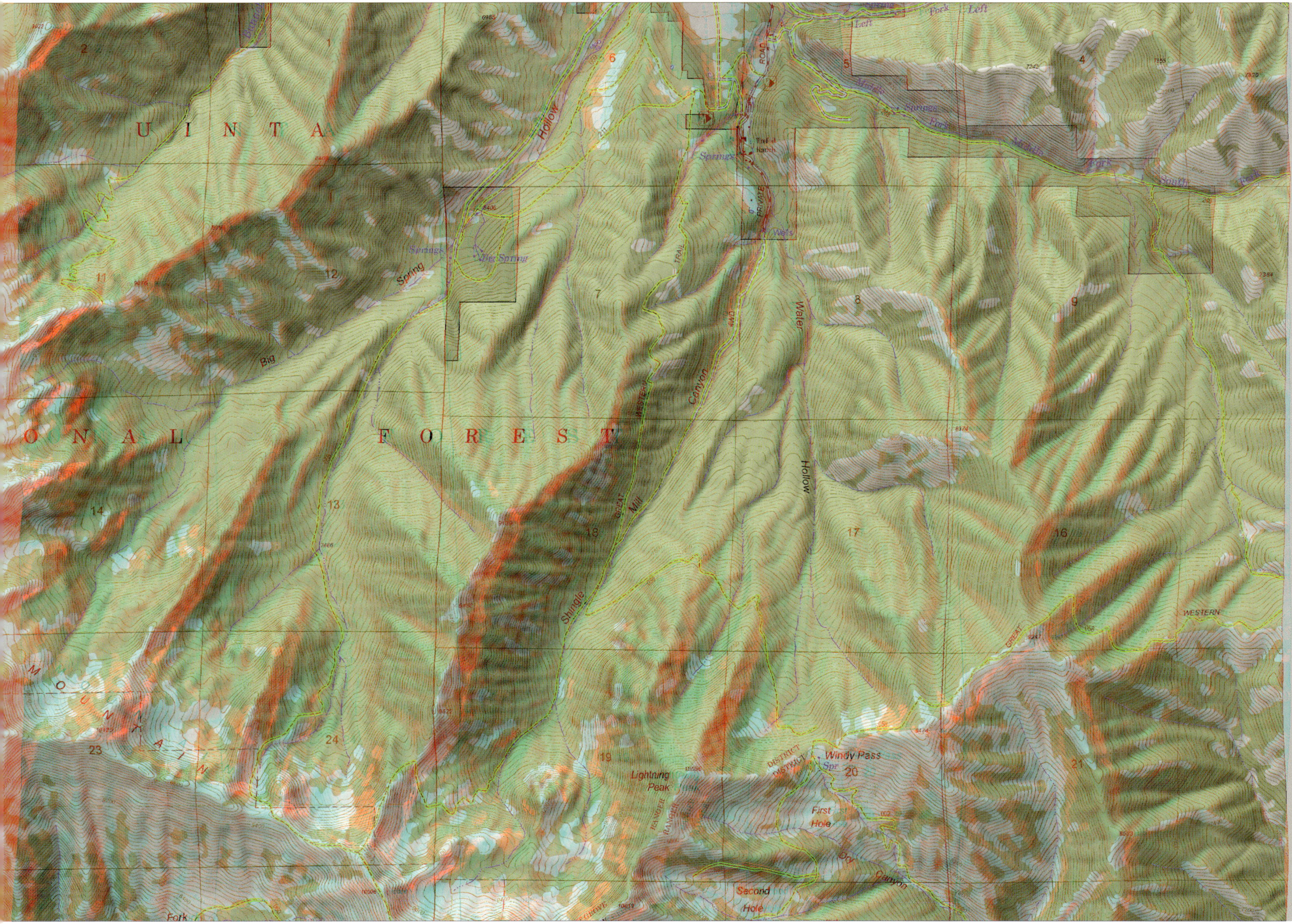

The anaglyph X displacement is 1175 feet (358 meters), centered at 7096 feet (2163 meters) between the low elevation of 5784 feet and the high elevation of 10480 feet (1763 to 3194 meters).

42	43
44	45
46	47

ADJACENT PAGES

N

SCALE 1 INCH = ½ MILE

0 ½ 1 MILE

0 1000 2000 3000 4000 FEET

0 0.5 1 KILOMETER

UTAH

Windy Pass

L R

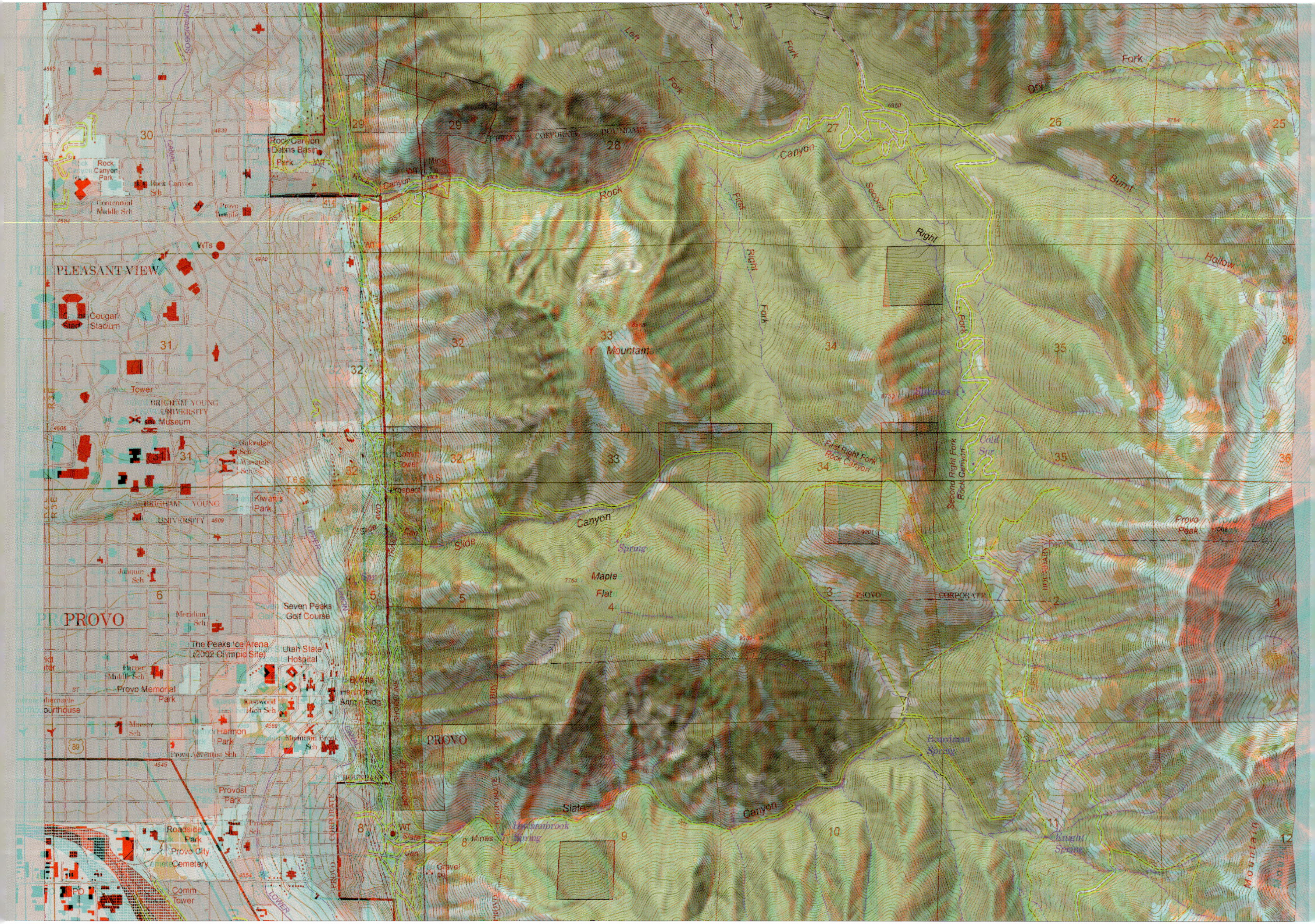
PLEASANT VIEW
PROVO
Cougar Stadium
BRIGHAM YOUNG UNIVERSITY
Museum
Kiwanis Park
Seven Peaks Golf Course
The Peaks Ice Arena (2002 Olympic Site)
Utah State Hospital
Provo Memorial Park
Provost Park
Roadside Park
Provo City Cemetery
Rock Canyon Park
Centennial Middle Sch
Rock Canyon
First Right Fork Rock Canyon
Second Right Fork Rock Canyon
Maple Flat
Slate Canyon
Provo Peak
Boardman Spring
Knight Spring
Burnt Hollow
Slide Canyon
Mountain

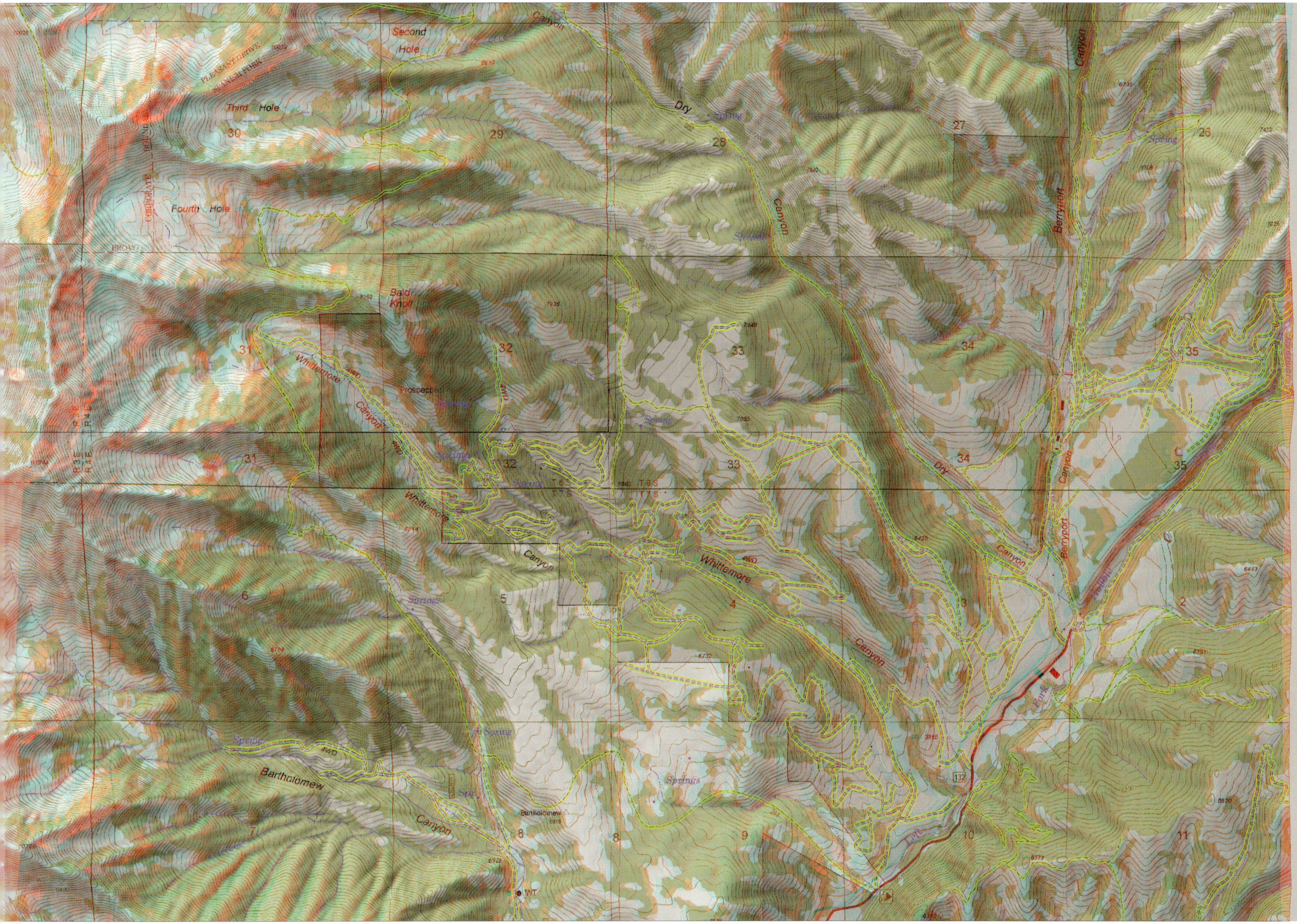

The anaglyph X displacement is 1381 feet (421 meters), centered at 7201 feet (2195 meters) between the low elevation of 5524 feet and the high elevation of 11048 feet (1684 to 3367 meters).

44	45
46	47

ADJACENT PAGES

N

SCALE 1 INCH = ½ MILE

0 ½ 1 MILE

0 1000 2000 3000 4000 FEET

0 0.5 1 KILOMETER

UTAH

Whittemore Canyon

L R

COMMON MAP SYMBOLS USED ON USGS QUADRANGLES:

BOUNDARIES

- County or equivalent
- Civil township or equivalent
- Incorporated city or equivalent
- Federally administered park, reservation, or monument (external)
- Federally administered park, reservation, or monument (internal)
- State forest, park, reservation, or monument and large county park
- Forest Service administrative area
- Forest Service ranger district
- National Forest System land status, Forest Service lands
- National Forest System land status, non-Forest Service lands
- Small park (county or city)

BUILDINGS AND RELATED FEATURES

- Building
- School; house of worship
- Athletic field
- Built-up area
- Racetrack or raceway
- Airport, paved landing strip, runway, taxiway, or apron
- Unpaved landing strip
- Well (other than water), windmill or wind generator
- Tanks
- Covered reservoir
- Gaging station
- Located or landmark object (feature as labeled)
- Roadside park or rest area
- Picnic area
- Campground
- Cemetery — Cem

CONTOURS

Topographic

- Index — 6000
- Intermediate

SURFACE FEATURES

- Disturbed surface

MINES AND CAVES

- Quarry or open pit mine
- Gravel, sand, clay, or borrow pit
- Mine tunnel or cave entrance
- Mine shaft
- Prospect
- Tailings — Tailings
- Mine dump

RIVERS, LAKES, AND CANALS

- Perennial stream
- Intermittent stream
- Perennial lake/pond
- Intermittent lake/pond
- Water well, geyser, fumarole, or mud pot
- Spring or seep

CONTROL DATA AND MONUMENTS

- U.S. mineral or location monument — USMM 438

Boundary monument

- Third-order or better elevation, with tablet — BM 9134
- Third-order or better elevation, recoverable mark, no tablet — 5628
- With number and elevation — 67 4567

Horizontal control

- Third-order or better, permanent mark — Neace
- With third-order or better elevation — BM 52
- With checked spot elevation — 1012
- Coincident with found section corner — Cactus
- Unmonumented

Vertical control

- Third-order or better elevation, with tablet — BM 5280
- Third-order or better elevation, recoverable mark, no tablet — 528
- Bench mark coincident with found section corner — BM 5280
- Spot elevation — 7523

LAND SURVEYS

Public land survey system

- Range or Township line
  - Location approximate
  - Range or Township labels — R1E T2N
- Section line
  - Location approximate
  - Protracted
  - Section numbers — 1 - 36
- Found section corner
- Found closing corner
- Witness corner — WC

Other land surveys

- Range or Township line
- Section line
- Land grant, mining claim, donation land claim, or tract
- Land grant, homestead, mineral, or other special survey monument

ROADS AND RELATED FEATURES

- Trailhead
- Interstate — 5
- U. S. — 101
- State — 79
- County — 6
- National Forest, suitable for passenger cars — 105, 61
- National Forest, suitable for high clearance vehicles — 105
- National Forest Trail — 384
- Primary highway
- Secondary highway
- Light-duty road
  - Composition: Unspecified
  - Paved
  - Gravel
  - Dirt
- Unimproved; 4 wheel drive — 4WD
- Trail
- Gate; Barrier

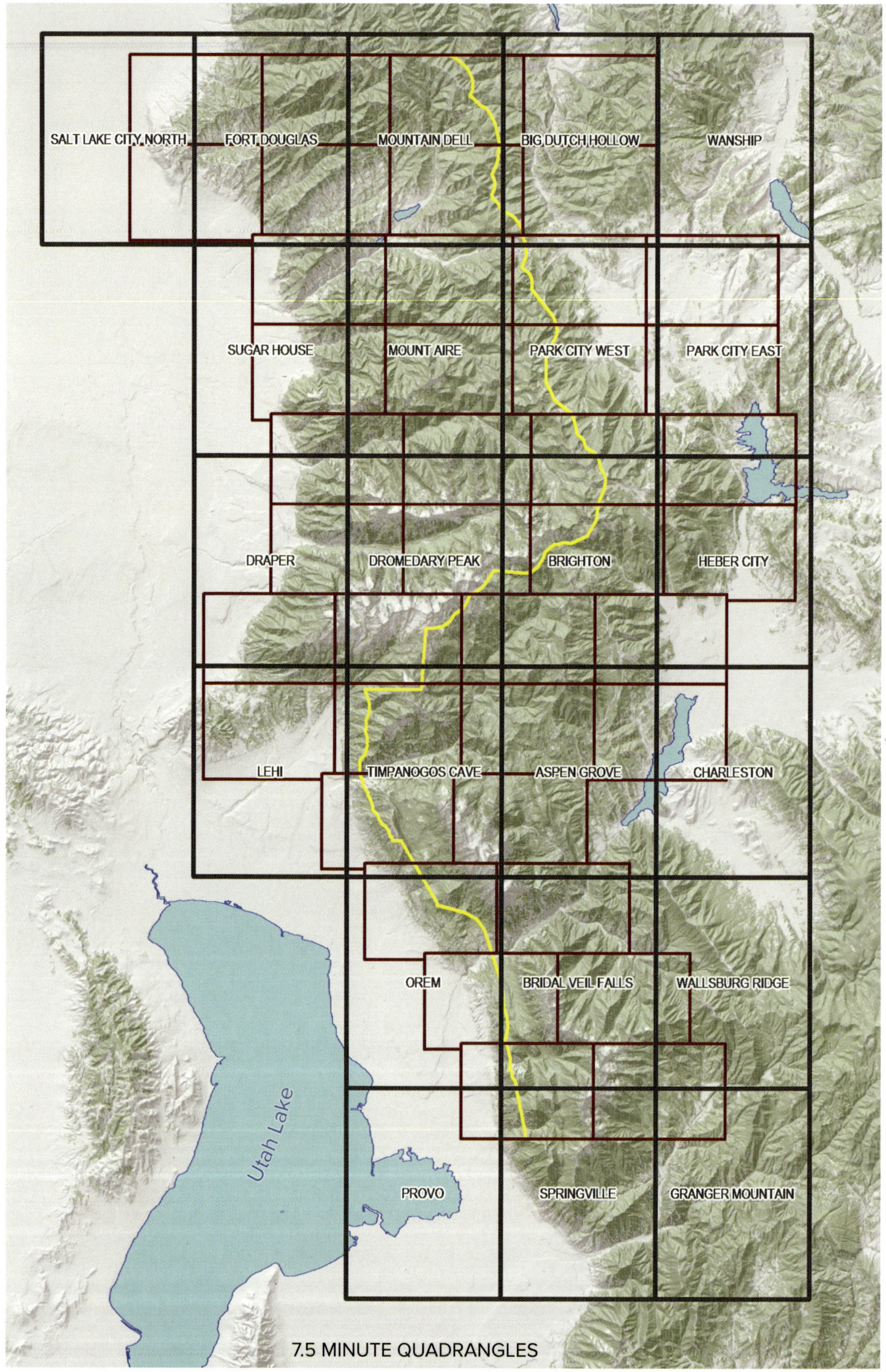